With Kindest Personal Regards
to
Frances and Brantley Davis
from
Florence and Eugene Fairbanks
February 1997

A SCULPTOR'S TESTIMONY IN BRONZE AND STONE

The Sacred Sculpture of
Avard T. Fairbanks

LEHI BLESSING HIS SON JOSEPH

A SCULPTOR'S TESTIMONY

IN

BRONZE AND STONE

The Sacred Sculpture

of

Avard T. Fairbanks

By

Eugene F. Fairbanks

ISBN# 0-916095-58-4

Printed in the U.S.A.

by Publishers Press

Salt Lake City, Utah

Acknowledgments

The author wishes to extend thanks to many who have contributed information and assistance for this publication. Many photographs were obtained from Mr. Lorin Wiggins and the Evans Sight and Sound Studios. The LDS Church Information Service has also been very helpful in obtaining other prints. Ortho R. Fairbanks has obtained information and photographs of sculpture at the Hawaiian Temple. Merwin G. Fairbanks has given considerable encouragement and helpful direction. Golden Larson has reviewed the manuscript and made constructive suggestions. Typing of the manuscript by Alice L. Hitz has also been of considerable assistance. Patience and sacrifice by my wife, Florence, and my family are deeply appreciated.

However, by far the greatest source of information and material was my father, Avard T. Fairbanks. Most of the photograhs printed were taken and developed personally by the sculptor. The photographs are his, unless otherwise specified.

One cannot conclude without remembering two great artists whose influence, even though they have departed, is deeply felt. My grandfather, John B. Fairbanks, and my uncle, J. Leo Fairbanks, have bestowed a dynamic appreciation in the family for masterpieces of art.

Eugene F. Fairbanks

Second edition acknowledgments

Editing and proof readings of second edition compositions have been performed by Philip R. Snider. Furthermore, he has also served as a consultant on scriptural accuracy and the literary quality of text. His advice and encouragement has been greatly appreciated.

TABLE OF CONTENTS

TABLE OF CONTENTS
(Continued)

LIST OF ILLUSTRATIONS

LIST OF ILLUSTRATIONS

LIST OF ILLUSTRATIONS

Dr. Avard T. Fairbanks, Sculptor

DR. AVARD T. FAIRBANKS, Sculptor
Biographical Sketch

Avard Tennyson Fairbanks was born in, Provo, Utah, on March 2, 1897, the tenth son in a family of eleven. His father, John B. Fairbanks, once a farm boy in a frontier village, had become one of the pioneer artists of the West. He had painted murals in several of the early Latter-day Saint temples. He was an instructor in art at the Brigham Young Academy (now Brigham Young University). To supplement the low income of teaching, he operated a photographic studio with the help of his oldest son, J. Leo. The mother of this large family, Lilly Annetta Huish Fairbanks, had intended to see that her children were well-educated, but an unfortunate accident prevented her from seeing her hopes fulfilled. She fell, injuring her back in August, 1897, and remained bedfast until she died eight months later. She left an infant son and several young children to be reared by the father, assisted by the teen-age children of the family.

A few years later, in 1902, an archeological expedition to Central America called the father away, and the family was managed by J. Leo, the oldest brother, and Annetta, the sister. Two years later, when the father returned to Utah, there appeared promise of opportunity in the wheat country of Canada. A move was made to a farm in Raymond, Alberta. However, this venture was beset with summer drouth and severe winter freezes. The family finances sank to a very low ebb. During one long, cold, dreary winter night, J. B. Fairbanks had a magnificent dream in which he was again creating great paintings on canvas. Believing this to be an omen, he decided again that he had a much greater future in art. That spring he moved his family back to Salt Lake City where he organized private instruction in art and again pursued creative painting. The family also operated a small farm which provided some basic necessities.

Avard first showed interest in sculpture at the age of twelve, when he modeled a pet rabbit under the direction of his brother, J. Leo, who by this time was an accomplished artist. He had studied in colleges and in Paris art schools. This clay rabbit was entered in the State Fair, and won a first prize. However, when the judge, a university professor, learned that it was the work of a boy, he refused to award the medal. This thoughtless act caused more than a disappointment. It made young Avard resentful and determined to do even better work. He resolved to become an accomplished artist so that the professor would in time recognize him as a sculptor. "I'll show him some day !" he said.

When his father went to New York City to make for private sale copies of masterpieces at the Metropolitan Museum, Avard soon followed. A permit, reluctantly granted because of youth, was obtained for him to copy sculpture at this institution. When the curator saw how well he did, he apologized for his reticence. A reporter one day observed his progress. Shortly a story appeared in the *New York Herald* titled, "Young Michaelangelo of this modern day in knickerbockers working at the Metropolitan Museum." This article attracted considerable attention, which led to other opportunities. He also modeled animals at the Bronx Zoological Gardens. He showed such ability that in 1910 and 1911 he was awarded scholarships to study at the Art Students League at New York under James Earl Fraser. During this time he became personally acquainted with several notable sculptors, often receiving advice and instruction from them. Among these were Herman A. McNeil, Cyrus E. Dallin, Adolph A. Weimar, Chester Beach, Gutzon Borglum, Solon Borglum, Paul Bartlett, A. Phimister Proctor and Larado Taft. At the Bronx Zoo he received technical assistance and criticism from Anna V. Hyatt and Charles R. Knight. The latter is famous for his restorations in sculpture of prehistoric animals. Young Fairbank's sculpture was displayed in the National Academy of Design when he was only fourteen years old. Payments for the copy work being done by his father were never regular and gradually dwindled. After a year and a half, it became necessary to return to Salt Lake City following a period of physical impoverishment amidst intellectual wealth. Avard has said that he knew what it was to be very poor. He also knew what it was to go hungry.

The father, recognizing the son's artistic ability, promoted a plan for further study in Paris. During the next two years, they tried to obtain sculpture commissions which might finance the trip. All efforts ended in disappointment until Avard offered to model a lion in butter for a creamery exhibit at the State Fair. This attracted a large crowd and the manager was well-pleased. A change in fortunes occurred as several other sales were made, assuring finances for the study abroad. A few other sales came in, sufficient to meet the anticipated expenses.

In 1913 he went to Paris to study at the Ecole Nationale des Beaux Artes, under Injalbert. While in Paris, he studied at the Ecole de la Grande Chaumiere, at the Academy Colarossi, and at the Ecole Moderne. His works were exhibited at the Grand Salon. Although he intended to continue in Paris, an adverse turn of events occurred—the outbreak of World War I. He and his father were sketching between school sessions in a small village near the Swiss border. News of the assassination of Archduke Ferdinand of Austria was followed by ominous rumors and reports. Each day a large number of the men of the village were called into military service and departed to join their units. In about three weeks, as mobilization progressed, it became imperative that Avard and his father return to the United States. Although the trip to the village by train had taken only four hours from Paris, it took over two days to return. Civilian travel was sidetracked and diverted for troop movement to the Alsace-Lorraine region. On arrival, the gay city of Paris was dismal. Shops of German proprietors had been ransacked by angry mobs. The taxis were gone, having been pressed into service for troop movement. Only a few horse-drawn hacks were available. Hurried arrangements were made to leave the city. Reser-

vations on a train to Calais were obtained. The morning of departure, they arose just before midnight and walked across Paris through the quiet, dimly lighted, narrow streets to the railroad station. They felt relieved as the train moved to the coast. However, the German army was advancing through Belgium. The train was diverted to Boulogne. Bridges were blown up after the train passed. This was the last train northwest from Paris. They obtained passage across the English Channel to Folkestone. There a considerate travel agent obtained two of the few remaining accommodations on a ship, the *Ansonia,* leaving Liverpool a few days later. He accepted as payment, without question, a check on a Salt Lake City bank. The voyage was stormy. The ship traveled off the usual course, with all lights off, since there was already concern about the submarine menace. As they arrived three days late, the view of the Statue of Liberty and New York Harbor was a welcome sight indeed. On debarkation, they had only fifteen cents. Credit was obtained by telegraph, which enabled them to proceed home by train.

They returned to Salt Lake City, where the young sculptor continued his high school education. During this time, he modeled pieces which were exhibited in the rotunda of the Fine Arts Palace of the Panama Pacific Exposition in San Francisco in 1915. His brother, J. Leo, and he received a commission to erect four sculptured friezes for the Latter-day Saint Temple in Laie, Hawaii. These were made of cast stone. Other sculpture included a bas relief honoring Hawaiian motherhood and a heroic statue of Lehi blessing Joseph.

While in Hawaii, he sent for his sweetheart, Maude Fox, of Taylorsville, Utah. They were married in Honolulu. Their honeymoon was a trip by interisland steamer to Hilo and a visit to the volcanos of Mauna Loa and Kiluea. When the sculpture was complete in 1918, they sailed for home, but the spirit of the islands had etched a lasting memory in their hearts.

Returning from the islands, he entered the University of Utah. Since he already had advanced training in art, he chose other, more academic, college courses. Military experience was included in the Student Army Training Program.

World War I ended, bringing the boys back home. He conceived an ambitious program of memorializing these men in heroic monuments. For the State of Idaho, he modeled a figure called "The Idaho

Doughboy," which was placed in two cities in that state. On a tour of the Northwest, he met Dean Lawrence of the School of Architecture at the University of Oregon. The dean was very impressed with his work and his training. An appointment as assistant professor of art was made in 1920 to teach sculpture at that institution in Eugene, Oregon. This was a challenging opportunity. Besides organizing sculpture courses on that campus, he also taught extension courses at Portland, Oregon.

His creative works while in Oregon included "The Awakening of Aphrodite," placed in the Washburn Gardens in Eugene. World War I memorials in bas relief were erected at Jefferson High School in Portland, and at Oregon State University in Corvallis. Bronze doors were placed at the United States National Bank in Portland. A relief panel titled "The Holy Sacrament" was placed at St. Mary's Cathedral in Eugene, Oregon. A portrait of Ezra Meeker, founder of The Old Oregon Trail Association, was modeled. Bronze monuments marking the Old Oregon Trail were placed in Baker and Seaside.

During 1924 he took a leave of absence to study at Yale University, where he was granted a Bachelor of Fine Arts degree. Returning to Oregon, he continued as an assistant professor until he was awarded a fellowship by the Guggenheim Foundation. This enabled him to go to Europe to study and do creative sculpture. By this time there were four boys in the family, the youngest of which was six months old. Many museums of cities in England, France, and Italy were visited, but Florence, Italy, the cradle of the Renaissance, was chosen for most of the study. Sculptures in the great galleries and beautiful cathedrals were often visited. Here he studied under one of the great contemporary Italian sculptors, Dante Sodini. He also studied at Scuola Fiorentina de Pittura. Creative sculpture included a fantasy of springtime, "La Primavera," carved in marble. A statuette honoring the Archiconfraternite Della Miseracordia was cast in bronze. This volunteer lay order in Florence, Italy, has for centuries been dedicated to assisting the infirm or injured townspeople. The "Pioneer Mother Memorial" for Vancouver, Washington, was also completed and cast in bronze at a Florentine foundry. Other creative sculpture included "Motherhood," a young mother nursing her infant. This also was carved in marble.

Returning to the United States in 1928, he taught at the Seattle Institute of Art. He studied art courses at the University of Washington in Seattle and in 1929 earned a Master of Fine Arts degree. He also completed one of his finest memorials, "The Ninetyfirst Division Monument," erected at Fort Lewis, Washington.

Moving the family to Ann Arbor, Michigan, in 1929, he joined the faculty of the University of Michigan as an associate professor of sculpture and resident sculptor in the newly established Institute of Fine Arts. There he organized a program of studies in sculpture. Annual sculpture exhibitions coincided with the May Festivals of music. In a few years, the hallways of University Hall were lined with the best works of students. He was called on frequently through the extension service to give demonstration lectures throughout the state of Michigan.

During the early years of the 1930 decade, commissions were scarce. He turned his attention to studies in the field of anatomy in the medical school. He was awarded a Master of Arts degree in 1933, and in 1936 a Doctor of Philosophy degree in anatomy. This led to an increased emphasis of anatomy in his teaching of sculpture. He was also able to give a greater expression to his sculptures, since he had done extensive dissection of facial musculature. In preparation for a doctoral thesis, many modeled reconstructions of the musculature of the head and neck as well as arms, legs, and torso were made. Plaster casts of these now hang on the anatomy laboratory walls at the University of Michigan, and the art departments of the University of Utah and Brigham Young University.

During the eighteen years of residence at Ann Arbor, Michigan, he was able to create many masterpieces. Prominent among these were "Winter Quarters Memorial" at Pioneer Mormon Cemetery, Florence, Nebraska; a monument placed in Grand Detour, Illinois, to honor Leonard Andrus, who, with John Deere, pioneered the steel moldboard plough; "Nebula," a fantasy garden figure, was exhibited at Northwest Flower Show in Detroit and again in 1939 at the New York World's Fair; "Rain," a fantasy also exhibited at the Northwest Flower Show, was selected along with works of America's greatest sculptors to be placed at Brookgreen Gardens in South Carolina; "Young Pegasus" was placed in Wilson's Meadowbrook Gardens in Rochester, Michigan. Other fantasies include "The Boy With the Shell," "Dawn and Morning Glories," "The Flower Girl," "Sunshine and Moonbeam," and "Aquarius the Water Bearer." Sacred sculpture included intaglio reliefs of the "Madonna and Child" and "Christ Among the Doctors" created for Mr. Frederick M. Zeder of Grosse Pointe, Michigan. For the Latter-day Saint display in the Hall of Religion at the Century of Progress World's Fair in Chicago, 1933, a sculptured relief panel was created and entitled "Eternal Progress." A pioneer group titled "Youth and New Frontiers," a companion piece to "A Tragedy of Winter Quarters," was exhibited at the Chicago World's Fair, 1934, and later placed in the Temple Square Museum, Salt Lake City, Utah.

Many portraits were made during this period. Prominent among these were the Right Honorable William Mackenzie King, prime minister of Canada; Honorable Gerry McGeer, mayor of Vancouver, British Columbia, a member of the Canadian House of Commons, and later a member of the Senate of the Canadian Parliament; Dr. G. Carl Huber, one of the world's eminent neuroanatomists, dean of the Graduate School, University of Michigan, and anatomy professor of the sculptor; a portrait of Mrs. Alexander G. Ruthven, wife of the president of the University of Michigan; Mrs. Helen Gardiner Phelan of Toronto, Canada; and Walter P. Chrysler, chairman of the Chrysler Corporation.

In addition to portraits of illustrious individuals, great monuments were in progress. "Lincoln the Frontiersman," a heroic figure of the vigorous railsplitter with a destiny, was modeled and cast. He created one of the great artistic portrayals of the "Emancipator." This bronze statue was erected in the courtyard of the Ewa Plantation School, Ewa, Hawaii, in 1944. Prominent on the North Dakota State Capitol grounds in Bismarck, is a heroic statue "The Pioneer Family" he erected honoring the pioneer family.

Besides the great monuments and the fantasy studies, animal studies were also created. "Puppy Love" and "A Little Bit Put Out" involved three puppies in a small box. Fine statuettes were modeled for the proud owners of Foremost High Flyer, a prize winning jersey bull, and Obuzier, a Percheron stallion of fame in his own realm.

As a contribution to industry, he designed an original radiator ornament, a ram, for the Dodge Motor Company, which was modified each year over two decades. A winged mermaid was created for the radiator ornament of the Plymouth in 1930, symbolic of floating power. A griffin of his design was chosen for the Hudson automobiles in 1933.

During World War II, as university enrollment decreased, and wishing to be of service to the nation, he accepted a position at the Ford Willow Run bomber plant in the personnel department. Following the war, industries began retooling for civilian needs. The American Society of Automotive Engineers, to meet urgent needs, sought his services in collaboration with the College of Engineering at the University of Michigan. This was a new venture for industry, art, and education, but Michigan is noted for its initiative in these fields. The teaching of automotive body design and styling was decided upon and courses were established with the extension division of the University of Michigan in the Rackham Educational Building in Detroit. His abilities as a designer were thus recognized by the greatest manufacturers of our day. When the automotive golden jubilee was celebrated in Detroit, under the direction of General Knudsen and George Romney, Dr. Fairbanks was called on to create the award, which he entitled "The Genius of Man, His Mind and His Works." Replicas were given to the living pioneers of the automotive industry in honor of their great services.

The University of Utah was expanding in the post-World War II period. Dr. Fairbanks was appointed dean and asked to organize a college of fine arts at this institution. He moved the family to Salt Lake City in 1947. An ambitious program was begun, with a new studio on the ground level. Here other examples of great statuary were created. Among these should be included the heroic bronze of Dr. Marcus Whitman, pioneer physician in the Pacific Northwest. This monument, placed in Statuary Hall in the nation's capitol to represent the state of Washington, has been heralded as one of the powerful and impressive studies of our day. Other memorializations in that hall of fame include Esther Morris of Wyoming, active in securing equal rights for women of that state. North Dakota is represented by his heroic bronze statue of John Burke, three times governor, for many years a Supreme Court justice, and treasurer of the United States during the administration of Woodrow Wilson. A monument was erected to the distinguished mining engineer, Daniel C. Jackling, who developed the Utah Copper Company, predecessor of Kennecott Copper, the greatest mining project ever undertaken by man. The statue was placed in the Utah State Capitol by the Kennecott Copper Corporation under the sponsorship of the Sons of Utah Pioneers. It is heroic in size and heroic in concept.

Other monuments to Lincoln were undertaken. A heroic bronze was erected in the restored New Salem Village in Illinois. This portrays the young, vigorous Abraham Lincoln in transition, at the crossroads of decision, resting his ax and picking up the law books. During Lincoln's years at New Salem, his living was earned by labor, but his developing interest was in public speaking. His future lay in law and politics. This monument was a gift of the Sons of Utah Pioneers. Another monument to Lincoln was erected at Lincoln Square in Chicago entitled "The Great Chicago Lincoln." At nearby Berwyn, Illinois, a monument in heroic bronze was placed entitled "Lincoln the Friendly Neighbor." This is a group portraying him as a friend to children of the neighborhood. Bas relief bronze panels commemorating the Lincoln-Douglas debates were erected at Knox College in Galesburg, Illinois. Marble portrait busts of Abraham Lincoln representing four ages—as a youth, the rail-splitter, the lawyer, and the president—were placed in the Ford Theater Museum in Washington, D.C.

Other monuments include "Guidance of Youth," erected in Bush Park, Salem, Oregon. One outstanding portrait study was a monumental bust of the oldest survivor of the Grand Army of the Republic, Albert Woolson, 107 years old. This work adorns the corridor of the City Hall of Duluth, Minnesota. Later Dr. Fairbanks was commissioned to create a monument to this man. It was placed on the Gettysburg battlefield. A bas relief panel honoring Anthony W. Ivins, active with youth and Boy Scout activities, was placed at Utah State University in Logan. Louis F. Moench, founder of Weber State University, Ogden, Utah, was memorialized by a bronze statue at that campus. Erected on the University of Utah campus is his representation in bronze of the "Ute Brave," a crouching Indian preparing to put an arrow to his bow.

Among his latest public monuments is one honoring Padres Dominguez and Escalante, explorers of Southwest United States, in 1676. The statue is erected in Spanish Fork, Utah.

Angel Moroni statues are erected on Temple Spires of several Latter-Day Saint Temples. A statue portraying the Mortal Moroni, was erected at Manti, Utah on the Temple grounds.

A monument honoring Nathan Woodbridge Ferris was erected on the campus of Ferris State College, Big Rapids, Michigan.

A portrait of Hamana Kalili, was modeled in 1937. He was a famous Hawaiian, a friend and foreman of construction during the building of the Hawaiian Temple of the Church of Jesus Christ of Latter-Day Saints. His portrait was cast in bronze and placed in Laie, Hawaii.

These many fine monuments have not interfered with modeling portraits of characters of eminence from various parts of the world. Among these may be noted:

Dr. Rufus B. von KleinSmid, chancellor of the University of Southern California;

Marshall Dana, chief editor of the *Oregon Journal*, regional planner, leader in National Reclamation Service, and prominent in public relations, in which capacity he was assistant to the president of the United States National Bank in Portland, Oregon;

Howard R. Driggs, formerly head of the Department of American Literature, New York University, and later president of the American Pioneer Trails Association;

Dr. Harvey Fletcher, formerly head of the Physics Department, Bell Telephone Laboratories, and professor at Columbia University, later professor of Physics at Brigham Young University, and dean of the Graduate School;

Dr. E. V. Kidder, chief archeologist, Carnegie Foundation, Washington, D.C.;

Dr. John A. Widtsoe, late apostle of The Church of Jesus Christ of Latter-day Saints, former president of both the Utah State Agricultural College and University of Utah;

Thomas J. Yates, scientist and theologian, former electrical engineer of Utah Power and Light Company, first director in the program establishing LDS seminaries and institutes:

James Moss, principal of Granite High School, father of United States Senator Frank Moss of Utah.

Roscoe Pound, eminent attorney and expert on Constitutional Law, Professor of Law, at the University of Nebraska, later Dean of Harvard Law School.

William Guy, Governor of North Dakota.

Reed O. Dingman, M.D., Professor of Surgery and Chairman of the Department of Plastic Surgery, University of Michigan, and a former student of Avard Fairbanks.

There are also many portraits of historic figures, which have been placed in prominent public locations.

A portrayal which is an excellent study and intimately felt is a study of his brother, Professor J. Leo Fairbanks, former supervisor of art for the public schools of Salt Lake City. He organized this city's first planning commission and later moved to Oregon State University where he was the chairman of the Department of Fine Arts.

The commander of the Phalanx of Knights of Thermopylae, Mr. Harris J. Booras, of Boston, Massachusetts, has collaborated with officials of the city of Sparta, Greece, to create and place there a memorial of heroic proportions to Lycurgus, the ancient lawgiver of that city. Nine centuries before Christ, this monarch established a constitutional government and created a senatorial system which granted a voice for the people, an intermediary between the king and his subjects. This was the first constitutional government in recorded history. The monument created by Dr. Fairbanks was erected in October, 1955, near the site of the ancient senate forum. It is near to the present Temple of Justice, the choicest location in Sparta, Greece.

The pony express has always been a topic of interest for historians. It has also captured the imagination of artists. A sketch of this subject was modeled in demonstration lectures before various groups during the Utah Centennial and a life size model was displayed in a parade in Salt Lake City. William Harrah of Reno, Nevada, who has taken a keen interest in history, par-

ticularly that which pertains to transportation, commissioned Dr. Fairbanks to create another heroic monument to the pony express and to its courageous young riders. This was erected and dedicated April 4, 1963, at Lake Tahoe. Mr. Harrah was so well-pleased that he ordered a duplicate to be placed in a museum to the pony express which he is developing at Reno, Nevada.

From among his small sculpture works may be noted the creation of medals of distinction. These include the "Washington Roebling Medal," given by the Mineralogical Society of America; "Appreciation Medal," given each year to the first citizen of Portland, Oregon; "Faith in Man and His Works," for the United States National Bank of Portland; "The Will to Achieve," for the Oregon Mutual Life Insurance Company (now the Standard Life Insurance Co.), Portland, Oregon; and the Utah Centennial emblem entitled "Vision and Our Heritage."

Another medal of worldwide importance, "Courage," was presented to Right Honorable Prime Minister Winston Churchill by former Right Honorable Prime Minister W. L. Mackenzie King during the Second World War, at a conference of the prime ministers of the Commonwealth of Nations of Great Britain. The same study was also presented to President Eisenhower by the Sons of Utah Pioneers shortly after his election. Another study in numismatic art is a plaque commissioned through the Medallic Art Company by the American Institute of Mining and Metallurgical Engineers, with a portrayal of Col. Daniel C. Jackling.

Recognition of outstanding doctors of medicine has been made by his bronze reliefs. Among these are: Dr. Harley Haynes, director of the University Hospital, Ann Arbor, Michigan; Dr. Fred Stauffer of Salt Lake City, in the Medical Arts Building; Dr. Maxwell Wintrobe, eminent hematologist at the University of Utah; Dr. Willard Richards, Bingham, Utah; Dr. John E. Bordley, Andelot Professor of Laryngology and Otology at Johns Hopkins University Medical School.

The demands of teaching and creative sculpture did not eclipse Avard Fairbanks' committment to his family. As the years went by, the family increased. Of eight sons, the first was born in Utah. After a move to Oregon, three more were born in Eugene. Following a year in Europe and Avard's appointment to the University of Michigan, the remaining four were born in Ann Arbor. Each son received instruction, personal attention and practical experience in modeling and casting.Finish work such as retouching and coloring was included in the training. Preparation for exhibits or placement of monuments became a part of the family enterprise. The boys were also taught photography, and had the opportunity to assist in photographic productions of sculpture.

Lectures and commissions often called the sculptor out of town, but sometimes part and occasionally all of the family would travel with him. Visits to Museums, historic points of interest, and National Parks would be included on the way. In fact, the boys traveled more than most of their classmates. Boy Scout work, camping, and out door activities, were an important part of family life.

Maude had always hoped for a daughter, but although she was disappointed, she remained undaunted. During a tour of Greece, following the dedication of the monument to Lycurgus at Sparta in 1955, she and Avard happened to visit an orphanage in that city. Maude's heart was moved when she saw many beautiful little girls. She wanted a daughter, and asked if she could adopt one or even two. The administrator said they would try to arrange it. It took several months to obtain the papers, but in time Avard and Maude received notification that a small girl would arrive at the Salt Lake City Airport. The seven year old arrived unattended, probably bewildered, but well cared for by the airline Hostess and happy. Three weeks later her eleven year old sister arrived. They adapted well to the family, and were readily accepted by their new brothers.

The girls were from a family of five children,living in Yerkion, Greece. Their grandfather had been killed after World War II when the Communists tried to take over Greece by fostering a revolution. Their Father had been killed later in an accident. The older children and mother survived on small jobs and by gleaning in the olive orchards. The opportunity for adoption was a sad but welcome relief to the family. As years passed, occasional letters were exchanged. Maria entered college, was soon married and started rearing a family. Georgia was able to visit her mother and brothers who had emmigrated to Australia. At another time during a trip to Greece, when accompanying her foster parents, she was able to visit her grandmother, who died soon afterwards at 105 years old, happy that her granddaughters had received fine care.

Besides the teaching of students in universities, Dr. Fairbanks has sought to extend the influence of fine art to the public by his demonstration lectures. These have been given to such diverse groups as secondary and high schools, garden clubs, professional women's clubs, medical societies, men's service clubs, art guilds, church groups, and college faculty meetings. He has appeared on television on several occasions.

During these presentations, the audience is surprised as the lecture changes from the formality of the introduction to the modeling with clay. After a few remarks, he slips off his suit coat, rolls up his sleeves, opens a suitcase, and dons a smock. Out of the suitcase next comes a modeling board with a floor flange bolted to one corner, a two-foot section of one inch gas pipe which he screws into the flange. A twelve-inch right angle section with a cluster of electric cables is screwed into this right angle. This wire armature he shows represents the framework of the figure, as he extends the wires for arms and legs. He makes this wire skeleton pose or dance or go through contortions for the amusement of the audience. As he begins to model, picking rolls of plasteline out of the suitcase, he discusses proportions of the body. He applies clay first, to give the figure a skull, the rib cage, and the pelvis. It assumes the appearance of a skeleton. Next muscles are applied. He mentions these by the anatomical name and describes their action. Shortly the figure assumes form, but appears grotesque. He then tells how the fatty tissues beautify the human form, filling the spaces and smoothing the lines as he adds more plasteline. Before a spellbound audience, the figure is progressively transformed from the skeleton stage to an anatomical study of muscle and bone. Moments later it assumes a human form. At this point he discusses the history of the personage to be modeled, the costume of the times, and more plasteline is applied to create clothing, with its folds and creases. Hair styling is also considered. Action and expression are given as he bends or twists the figure to give it more life and motion. He relates bits of art history as it progresses from the stiff, expressionless Egyptian figures, to the Greeks who gave movement, and to the Renaissance Italians where emotion and expression were added. As he starts to do the finer details of the face, even though working rapidly, he expresses regret that time does not permit the refinements of a more complete study. He relates some of the individual features of the portrayed character, as well as the personality, the hopes, and the ambitions manifest. He often quotes from famous writings and speeches. At the conclusion, he reaches into the suitcase, lifting out a drape which he places around the base. This little touch gives the statuette the appearance of a piece ready for exhibit.

He concludes by relating the further processes necessary for completed statuary. This includes plaster casting, bronze casting, or carving in marble. After the lecture a crowd invariably gathers for a closer view. Many who have watched are encouraged toward artistic achievement.

In 1965 Dr. Fairbanks was called to the University of North Dakota as special consultant in fine arts and resident sculptor. He has given many demonstration lectures throughout that state. There he has produced an impressive study in sculpture titled "Alma Mater."

During his professional career Dr. Avard Fairbanks has had many honors bestowed upon him. He is a fellow of the National Sculpture Society, a member of the Architectural League of New York, a member of the International Institute of Arts and Letters, and an honorary member of the Society of Oregon Artists. He is a member of Circolo Delgi Artisti di Firenzi (Florence, Italy). He has been made a member of the Protetore Della Contrada Della Torre da Siena, Italy. The National Sculpture Society granted Dr. Fairbanks the Herbert Adams Memorial Medal for distinguished service to American sculpture.

He was awarded a medal of the Knights of Thermopylae by King Paul of Greece at the ancient battle site where Leonidas and three hundred Spartans fought to their death against King Xerxes and the army of ten thousand Persians. From Lincoln College at Lincoln, Illinois, he received an honorary degree of doctor of fine arts. The Lincoln Memorial University in Harrogate, Tennessee, has conferred upon Dr. Fairbanks their highest recognition, the Lincoln Diploma of Honor. Another very outstanding recognition which he has received is the Lincoln Medal of the Sesquicentennial Commission of the Congress of the United States.

In addition to these many recognitions, there is a constant desire to create additional great masterpieces of art. The great artists of past ages left lasting influences on their cultures. Dr. Fairbanks hopes to create and produce many more heroic and important works which will reflect the civilization and culture of our times.

Since much of Dr. Fairbank's effort was directed toward teaching sculpture in universities, a review is incomplete without a few quotations of his thoughts and philosophy of art.

"The arts are created for contemplation and edification, the expression of the highest ambitions and the spiritual hope of a people. These produce a culture that lives on to uplift subsequent generations. The influential cultural periods came about in times when men with understanding, with technical skills, and with high purpose were willing and ready to put their ideals into form. We are now on the verge of a great civilization. We may say we have opportunities for a new golden age of art."

"A sculptor must comprehend a significant civilization, one that is indicative of intellectual advancement of the times in which he lives. The hope of the world lies in our faith and in our spiritual ideals. Such ideals we express in material form. If we possess these and strive vigorously for the accomplishment of these, we will produce a great culture. Our civilization should not be contained in material welfare only. Nor should all sorts of frivolity and fanfare creep in and become our objective. For the great inspiration comes to souls whose thoughts turn in the direction of the eternal things of life."

"To be sure, art must be intellectual and must therefore have a thoroughgoing terminology, technical—in accord with scientific terms—and philosophical as well. However, instead of being vague and occult, with the intent of mystification, art must clarify and be simple and direct in its purposes. It should be understandable to children, the untutored, as well as to the most highly learned and technically trained. When our work is erected in public places for all to behold, we build an atmosphere and an environment. For this reason, masterpieces of sculpture, because of their very nature of attracting attention, evoke admiration. Our products therefore become great factors in large-scale education and community uplift and pride."

"Our kind of work is one dealing primarily with order. Thus it is a process of organization and coordination. The adjustments and arranging of dissimilars into unity and unification and the expression of the universals into material have a way of giving soul to substance. All who see our works in the varying moods of weather see them thus standing solid and firm and undaunted. Observers are able to sense their meanings and know of those ideals of which they bespeak."

"Through simple harmonies, art can bring understanding and uplift to the downtrodden. It can recognize the finer qualities of men of all stations of life and cause people to believe their own kind of living is worthwhile, particularly since art ennobles the struggles of life. We who are given the powers to express these must sense the problems of life in its many conditions and express them through our various media, thus enabling our deep, soul-felt concepts and feelings to have real and tangible form."

"Along with social and domestic and the varying personal things of life, art too must have deep concern in the industrial progress, religious inspirations, and political programs. Because art itself theoretically is striving to achieve a harmony in the total of a composition, the principles involved can be systematized in writing and in diagrammatic patterns. And as scientific principles have become important formulae, so too our art principles of harmony can be utilized in formulae for social adjustments and international diplomacy."

During the eighth decade of his life, Avard T. Fairbanks continued with enthusiasm to create fine sculpture. In addition to his creative endeavours, he spent much of his life teaching, and it was not surprising that he invited grandchildren to his studio that they might continue the artistic tradition of the family. He also made several trips to Pietrasanta, Italy to the marble carving studios to finish his portraits and fantasy sculpture. Sometimes his sons or grandsons would accompany him.

The marble carvers expressed admiration for his ability as an artist, and his energy and stamina through long days of work. They encouraged him to order more pieces to be finished. The letters he wrote home expressed a sense of satisfaction tempered with loneliness. He had come to love the Italian people and the countryside of the Carrara Mountains and the Italian Riviera; but during six week marble carving ses-

sions, in which he worked long hours, he would miss his wife and family.

Some of his later significant statues were cast in Italy where he could arrange for the assistance of technicians and facilities for three dimensional enlargement. At an age when other men were enjoying leisure pursuits, Avard Fairbanks continued to create great monuments and portraits. When not modeling with clay, he was drawing plans for other statuary.

After Dr. Fairbanks reached mandatory retirement age, the sculpture studio, where he had created many heroic monuments, was no longer available to him. It had been a makeshift arangement in a building at Fort Douglas originally erected for a military truck repair shop. As the University of Utah expanded, the building was scheduled for demolition.

The studio which he obtained after University retirement, served him many years. He had moved his sculpture and equipment into a building which was formerly a temporary airport warehouse, built during World War II. The facilities, however, were too small for creation of heroic statuary. This building was also intermittently scheduled for demolition as plans for the airport expansion waxed and waned. The rooms were filled with books, plans, drawings, and sculpture which many art collectors would consider priceless. In addition, there were tools, molds, materials, and photographic equipment. He even did marble carving with pneumatic carving tools.

Eventually a deadline was set for demolition of the building. The task of moving seemed formidible to one past the his prime of his physical strength. However, family members converged from distant cities, found a new location and made the move involving many truckloads. He remarked how he envied the vigor of his sons, yet in the next breath he would tell of great plans for a hall of heroic statuary. His last plan was for a sacred, biblical subject, John, the Revelator, receiving a vision.

A few days before Christmas 1986, he was rushed to the hospital with a heart attack. As he was improving, he renewed his optimism and continued formulating plans for the monument. He even asked a friend to arrange for about a ton of clay. On New Years Day, another attack occurred and his heart did not respond to treatments. He died just two months short of ninety years.

Avard Tennyson Fairbanks was survived by his wife and a great posterity. Avard and Maude had eight sons and two adopted daughters. A brief description of their training and professions in chronological order is appropriate.

Avard Fox Fairbanks, earned BS and MS degrees in Engineering at the University of Michigan, and became an Aerospace Engineer, in the California aircraft industry.

Eugene Fox Fairbanks was awarded BA and MD degrees at the University of Michigan. He was certified by the American Board of Anesthesiology and the American Board of Family Practice, and he practiced anesthesiology and family practice in Bellingham, Washington.

Elliott Aldron Fairbanks was granted BA degree and MA degree from the University of Utah. He specialized in Sculpture and later in Academic administration as a dean at the College of Eastern Utah. He later transferred his talents to industrial administration with the Unisys Corporation.

Justin Fox Fairbanks earned BA and MA degrees from the University of Utah, studying Sculpture. After working with his father, he was appointed Professor of Art, Eastern Arizona College. He has been commissioned for many creative sculptures.

Virgil Fox Fairbanks earned a BA degree at the University of Utah, and an MD degree at the University of Michigan. He was certified by the American Board of Internal Medicine, and developed special interest in hematology. He was appointed as a Hematologist at the Mayo Clinic, Rochester, Minnesota.

Jonathan Leo Fairbanks, earned a BA degree in Art at the University of Utah, and an MA degree at the University of Pennsylvania. He chose to be a portrait painter, and developed interest in colonial art. He was a curator at the Henry Francis Du Pont Winterthur Museum in Delaware, and became the author of books on colonial antiquities. He was later appointed a Curator of American Decorative Arts and Sculpture at the Boston Museum of Fine Arts.

David Nathaniel Fox Fairbanks earned a BA degree and a MD degree at the University of Utah. He was certified by the American Board of Otolaryngology. Pursuing a career in academic medicine, he was appointed Professor of Surgery and Chairman of the Department of Otolayngology at the George Washington University Medical School, Washington, D.C.

Grant Ruthven Fairbanks earned a BA degree and an MD degree at the University of Utah. He was certified by the American Board of Surgery and the American Board of Plastic Surgery. He practices plastic surgery at St. Marks Hospital, Salt Lake City, Utah.

Avard and Maude Fairbanks were also very proud of their adopted daughters. Maria Fairbanks Hanson, housewife and mother of seven children, is married to Bret Hansen an aerospace engineer. They reside in Simi, California.

Georgia Fairbanks earned a BA degree at the University of Utah, studying music. She is an Instructor in Voice, Salt Lake City High Schools.

Dr. Fairbanks was also survived by more than fifty grandchildren and more than forty great grand children. Several family members have chosen art as a career. A nephew, Ortho Fairbanks, is a professional sculptor and has taught Art at the L.D.S. Church College of Hawaii, at Laie and at Holbrook College in Holbrook, Arizona. Two grandaughters, Teressa and Hillary Ann have studied Art and Museum Science in Massachusetts. Another grandson, Daniel Fairbanks, a plant geneticist and professor on the faculty at Brigham Young University, has demonstrated a keen interest and talent in sculpture, and has been commissioned to create some fine statuary. Many grandchildren have chosen health science and other fields of endeavour, with art as an avocation.

The influence and inspiration of the art of Avard Fairbanks have touched the lives of his many students, a number of whom have chosen to teach art or have succeeded at professional careers in sculpture.

This book would appear incomplete without a quotation from Dr. Fairbanks' first instructor, his mentor and his oldest brother, J. Leo Fairbanks, a sculptor and painter of renown. For many years he was the chairman of the Art Department of Oregon State College at Corvallis, Oregon. His "Creed" gives one pause for thought.

Creed

Art is for service; for making things beautiful as well as useful;

for lifting men above the sordid things that grind and depress:

to give a joyous optimism in one's work;

to realize, during one's leisure, the ideals that have been contemplated in one's most precious moments;

to take pleasure in seeing beauty as it exists in what man has made as well as in one's immediate environment;

to see all the ideal in the real;

and to realize transistory hopes in enduring tangible material.

To me, the purpose of art is to visualize ideals, to realize ideals, and to idealize realities.

J. Leo Fairbanks

GOD SO LOVED THE WORLD

For God so loved the world, that he gave his only begotten Son, that whosoever believeth in him should not perish, but have everlasting life. For God sent not his Son into the world to condemn the world, but that the world through him might be saved.

John 3: 16-17

In him was life; and the life was the light of men.

John 1: 4

And the world was made by him, and the world knew him not.

He came unto his own, and his own received him not. But as many as received him, to them gave he power to become the sons of God, even to them that believe on his name.

John 1: 10-12

God So Loved the World

13

MARY AND THE INFANT JESUS

And I looked and beheld the virgin again, bearing a child in her arms. And the angel said unto me: Behold the Lamb of God, yea, even the Son of the Eternal Father!

(1 Nephi 11:20-21)
Book of Mormon

Mary and the Infant Jesus

THE HAWAIIAN TEMPLE SCULPTURE

Although the Latter-day Saint temple in Laie, Hawaii, is one of the smallest of the many temples, it is held to be one of the most beautiful. Much of the beauty is attributed to the simple yet harmonious design. It is greatly enhanced by the superb landscape gardening, by the colonnades of palm trees that rustle with the trade winds, and by the lush tropical vegetation. Yet, in addition, much can be said for the sculpture which adds the human touch and also gives a message with profound and moving appeal.

The four friezes were planned largely by J. Leo Fairbanks, the older brother who was not only a fine painter but also a scholar of the Bible and the Book of Mormon. Much of the symbolism and arrangements of figure groups were first sketched out on J. Leo's drawing board. The two brothers worked together designing and modeling in clay, often referring to historical texts and the sacred scriptures in order to portray details as accurately as might be done. Scale models were first made, from which the enlarged full-size sculpture was completed. The final work of casting and placement on the temple in Laie was under the direction of Avard Fairbanks.

The decorative friezes at the cornice of the central section are sculptured in near life-size and finished in cast stone. Each of the four is symbolic of great periods of time called dispensations of the gospel in sacred literature. Altogether there are one hundred twenty-three figures representing important characters.

West Frieze

The west frieze depicts the great leaders and prophets in the dispensation recorded in the Old Testament. In the center is Adam in the Garden of Eden between the tree of life and the tree of knowledge of good and evil. Behind him are radiant beams of light symbolic of the Spirit of God directing his chosen leaders on earth. At Adam's right is Eve holding a child and kneeling before the altar of sacrifice. Behind the altar Cain cowers in a cloak; his sacrifice of fruit of the field was rejected by God, while Abel's offering, a blood sacrifice of the first of the flock, was respected. Cain in wrath slew his brother Abel. The remaining figures to the right of Adam are patriarchs. First is Seth, the son of Adam. Next is Enoch, who "walked with God." Noah holds a dove with an olive twig symbolizing deliverance from the flood. Slightly behind and to Noah's right is Melchizedek, the king-priest of Salem who blessed Abram. Isaac is portrayed as a boy carrying the wood for his own sacrifice as his Father Abraham hearkens to the voice of God and regretfully prepares the sacrifice which God later forbade him to make.

The Hawaiian Temple

The Church of Jesus Christ of Latter-day Saints

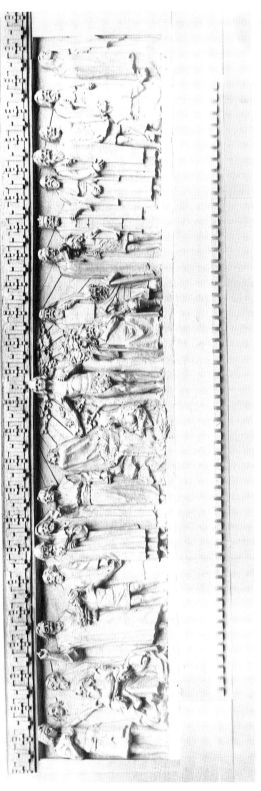

West Frieze, Hawaiian Temple, portraying the Old Testament

The group of figures at the end of the frieze, to the right of Adam, represents Jacob with his sons Judah, Benjamin in the background, and Joseph who was sold into slavery, wearing Egyptian dress. He appears startled, suggesting to his father that he should not cross his arms in blessing his grandchildren, Ephraim and Manasseh, who kneel at Jacob's side. By placing his right hand on Ephraim's head, and the left hand on Manasseh, the firstborn, Jacob explains that while Manasseh will become a great people, Ephraim will become even greater than he and Ephraim's seed will become a multitude of nations.

To the left of Adam is a group representing judges, kings, and prophets of the Old Testament. First is Moses, seated, holding a staff in one hand and the tablets of the laws in the other. Behind him stands Aaron, clothed in the robe of his priestly office. Kneeling and

bowed is Joshua, who succeeded Moses, led the children of Israel into the promised land, and captured Jericho. Samuel the prophet, is shown anointing the young David, who became King of Israel. King Solomon the wise is next, and to his left are three prophets, Elijah, Isaiah, and Jeremiah. Daniel is represented kneeling, pleading for the release of Israel from the captivity of Babylon, and Ezekiel the prophet stands behind. The last figure is symbolic representing the children of Israel; it is a woman mourning and looking out hopefully for the promised Savior.

South Frieze

Facing the south is a frieze portraying persons and events prominent in the New Testament, including Christ, his ministry, and the establishment of his Church.

18

South Frieze, portraying the New Testament

The central figure is Jesus; at his extreme right (observer's left) are Joseph of Nazareth, Mary, and a shepherd who, with his lamb, gazes upward at the Messiah. Next to the shepherd in the foreground sits a beggar whose sight was restored, and the woman taken in sin. The woman was to have been stoned, but Jesus came and said, "Let him who is without sin cast the first stone." Behind these seated figures are Andrew and Simon leaving their boats and nets at the Sea of Galilee to become "fishers of men." The standing figure with outstretched left arm is John the Baptist calling the faithful to repent. Kneeling in front is a devout believer offering a prayer in humility. To the right of Jesus is a group in crouched positions portraying afflicted persons: the sick, the halt, and the blind. Holding to his robe is a small child, which emphasizes his words, "Suffer little children, and forbid them not, to come unto me: for of such is the kingdom of heaven." Behind the afflicted persons are Jesus' beloved disciples, James and John.

To the left of Jesus stands Peter, with sword partly drawn from the scabbard. Jesus is restraining Peter, who has just cut off an ear of the high priest's servant (figure not portrayed). Behind Peter is a Roman soldier who attended the crucifixion, while in the foreground Cornelius kneels, seeking baptism by Peter. Saul of Tarsus, arising from the earth, covers his eyes with his hands in blindness; the figurative rays in the background representing the light from heaven at his conversion near the gates of Damascus. A group portrays the missionary labors of Silas with a companion and the growth of the Church of Christ through the new converts shown kneeling. The seated figure with the crown represents Constantine and his imperial edict of Milan, which gave respect and protection to the Christian Churches. This is followed by figures portraying events leading to the Protestant reformation, such as the purchase of indulgences, while a seated figure labors to translate the Bible from Greek and Latin into the language of the people.

19

North Frieze

The frieze on the north face of the temple represents the important events and outstanding personages on the American continent which are recorded in the Book of Mormon.

The central figure is that of Christ; to his extreme left (observer's right) is Lehi, a prophet of Israel, who in 600 B.C. foretold the coming of the Messiah and the destruction of Jerusalem. He and his family fled into the wilderness and eventually crossed the Pacific Ocean to the Americas. He is sculptured holding ancient Hebrew scriptures, the Brass Plates of Laban, secured before their departure. To his right is a small boy, his youngest son Joseph, to whom Lehi gave a great blessing and prophecy. The two opposing figures to Lehi's right are Nephi, his fourth son, a stalwart, righteous, young leader who succeeded his father; and Laman, a rebellious son who rejected Nephi's leadership and chose a path of wickedness. From these two sons descended two great nations, often in conflict that eventually culminated in a terrible civil war. The greater portion of the Book of Mormon recounts events of these two nations over a period of a thousand years.

Generally the Nephites were a righteous, industrious people, while the Lamanites, cursed with a dark skin, were rebellious and belligerent. However, among the Nephites were some who indulged in wicked deeds. One of these was King Noah, a despot shown seated, wearing a crown and holding a goblet. Seated on the ground is Alma, a prophet who preached righteous living and led a rebellion against King Noah. The old stooped man seated holding a sword is Coriantumr, last survivor of a nation called the Jaredites, whose ancestors fled from old Babylon during the confusion of tongues and the destruction of the Tower of Babel. They came to the Americas several centuries prior to the Nephites. The Book of Mormon also contains a record of these people.

The archer standing over a fallen warrior portrays the many armed conflicts between Lamanites and Nephites. Behind him is a banner held by Moroni, a Nephite leader whose army waged a successful campaign against the Lamanites. The banner's inscription admonishes, "In memory of our God, our religion, and freedom, and our peace, our wives and children."

Yet there were some among the Lamanites who chose the path of righteousness. Samuel the Lamanite was the most prominent of these. He became a prophet and foretold by revelation through an angel the coming of the Savior to the earth and to the peoples on the American continent. He also admonished them towards a course of repentance and faith and righteousness, to avert destruction. He is shown facing a star and looking towards Christ. Kneeling in the foreground is a man with feathered headdress and a woman with peaceful intent, after conversion, as they listen to a Nephite missionary facing them.

The central figure of Christ is shown between columns symbolic of the culture on the American continent. He is portrayed during his ministry among the Nephites, after his resurrection and before his ascension. His visitation to these people substantiates his statements during his Palestinian ministry: "Other sheep I have, which are not of this fold." The account of his teachings to the Nephites is one of the most beautiful, expressive, and significant passages in sacred literature, chapters eleven to twenty-six of Third Nephi.

A kneeling figure on the Savior's right is Nephi III, a devoted follower of Jesus, shown pleading with his people to heed the Lord's teachings. Many believed and they are typified by the three figures kneeling in the foreground. Behind them stands a haughty group who rejected the doctrines, represented by a robber, a murderer, and an anti-Christ. The figure in a boat is Hagoth, a builder of large ships which he launched into the west sea on the borders of the land Bountiful by the land Desolation. He took two groups of Nephites to the land north and did not return. It has been thought that Polynesians descended from him and his followers. Beside the boat stand two Hawaiians looking at a record of these ancient Americans for some information about their ancestors. A figure representing Columbia, the United States, lends a protecting hand over the Hawaiian people. Before them is seated Mormon, the leader of the last of the Nephites, who tried in vain to exhort them to righteous living. He was their general in battle with the Lamanites and finally was an historian. He took the extensive records of his people and abridged and compiled them into the records inscribed on the plates of gold from which the Book of Mormon was translated. The records were completed by his son Moroni, shown as the last figure to the extreme right (observer's left) of the Savior. At the time of the complete destruction of the Nephites, Moroni concealed these records in the Hill Cumorah where they remained until they were revealed to Joseph Smith by the Angel Moroni.

North Frieze, portraying the Book of Mormon

The Church of Jesus Christ of Latter-day Saints

21

East Frieze

The frieze facing the east portrays opening events of the present or latter-day dispensation of the gospel, described in holy scriptures as the dispensation of the "fullness of times." The teachings and work of the Church in this dispensation are also symbolized in sculpture.

One sees the figure of a boy kneeling in supplication. This represents Joseph Smith, a youth confused by the intolerance and religious clamor of his time, at about 1820 in a community near Palmyra, New York. One day, while studying the Bible in order to seek a solution to the conflict of opinions, he came upon the fifth verse of the first chapter of the Epistle of James: "If any of you lack wisdom, let him ask of God, that giveth to all men liberally and upbraideth not; and it shall be given him. But let him ask in faith, nothing wavering." The meaning of this passage struck him to the heart and after pondering this message he resolved to ask of God. One morning he retired to the woods to pray in solitude. As an answer to prayer, he received a vision, a glorious manifestation in which two living heavenly beings, the Father and the Son, appeared to him, spoke with him, answered his questions, and gave him counsel. They are represented by the central figures. The more venerable could be saying: "This is my Beloved Son. Hear Him !"

Other visions to this young man followed, the next about three years later, again in response to a humble prayer. The Angel Moroni, the same person shown on the Book of Mormon frieze, appeared as a resurrected being and told of events past and events to come. It was Moroni who later delivered to Joseph Smith the ancient record inscribed on plates of gold and buried in a vault in the Hill Cumorah. After translation it was known as the Book of Mormon. The Angel Moroni is shown holding the ancient records and standing to the right of the central figure.

Faith, the first principle of the gospel, is also demonstrated by Joseph Smith. Repentance, the second principle, is symbolized by a kneeling young woman deep in thought, while the third principle, baptism by immersion for the remission of sins, is portrayed by two figures in a baptismal font. Overhead is a dove, spoken of in the Gospel of St. Luke as the Spirit

the Holy Ghost which descended upon Christ when he was baptized by John the Baptist. Here it symbolized the bestowal of the gift of the Holy Ghost under the hands of those having authority.

The figures of two men laying hands upon the head of another is symbolic of the restoration of the priesthood to the earth. This was restored by John the Baptist when he appeared in a vision to Joseph Smith and Oliver Cowdery. The priesthood of Melchizedek was restored through Peter, James, and John in a later vision to Joseph Smith and Oliver Cowdery. A person dressed in the flowing robes of biblical times stands in the background looking on. This symbolizes the priesthood that was restored by the authority of those who held it anciently and is the foundation today of The Church of Jesus Christ of Latter-day Saints.

Further to the right of the central group are figures representing administration of the sacrament of the Lord's Supper, taken in remembrance of the Savior.

At the extreme right of the frieze is a figure representing an angel spoken of in The Revelation of St. John, chapter fourteen, verses six and seven. "And I saw another angel fly in the midst of heaven, having the everlasting gospel to preach unto them that dwell on the earth, and to every nation, and kindred, and tongue, and people, Saying with a loud voice, Fear God, and give glory to him; for the hour of his judgment is come: and worship him that made heaven, and earth, and the sea, and the fountains of waters."

At the left of the central group a man is seated studying genealogy. He is searching out names of his ancestors in order that he might have such sacred earthly ordinances as baptism by authority of the restored priesthood performed for them in the temple. In this way, his ancestors too may benefit in the spirit world from certain blessings which may not have been available during their stay on earth.

Through the authority of the priesthood, which has power to bind in heaven whatsoever is bound on earth, marriages and family relationships are sealed for eternity in Latter-day Saint temples. These ordinances may be done vicariously for the dead who in life may not have had the opportunity. The keys for temple work were given to leaders of The Church of

East Frieze, portraying the latter-day dispensation of the gospel

Jesus Christ of Latter-day Saints by Elijah in a vision at the temple at Kirtland, Ohio, in 1937, as foretold in Malachi 4:5-6: "Behold, I will send you Elijah the prophet before the coming of the great and dreadful day of the Lord." The four figures in the background represent a family so united in the spirit world through vicarious temple ordinances.

To the left of this group are two kneeling figures laying hands on the head of someone ill; this represents those holding the priesthood administering to the sick. Next is a kneeling woman holding a basket. She represents the Relief Society, a Church auxiliary which renders help to those in need and also affords women social, cultural, and educational programs. Another auxiliary, the Sunday School, is represented by a teacher with a child. Other important auxiliaries are the Young Men's and Young Women's Mutual Improvement Associations, which promote social, recreational, and intellectual achievement in the youth. The figure of a man holding a sheaf of grain in one hand

and a purse in the other is a worker, a wage earner and head of a family, fulfilling the financial law of the Church by the payment of the tithe of one's yearly increase. To his left is a standing figure robed in academic cap and gown, while a seated figure in the foreground works at a spinning wheel. These figures represent two important precepts of the Church, education and industry.

A young man holding a satchel represents a young man leaving his family and home to go on a mission for about two years to one of the many missions throughout the nations of the world. Approximately twelve thousand such young men and women are constantly engaged in missionary effort, preaching the gospel at the expense of themselves or their families.

The final group portrays a young family, the husband and wife united by temple marriage for time and all eternity, with a child, symbolizing the Latter-day Saint teachings of the divinity of motherhood and the sanctity of the home.

23

LEHI BLESSING HIS SON JOSEPH

Behind the temple stands the statue of Lehi blessing his youngest son Joseph. It is erected in a secluded courtyard enclosed by a tall hedge. There is such a sense of serenity and awe in its presence that people naturally speak in low tones while viewing it. Yet there is no sanctimonious effect. The figure of Lehi, though once vigorous, shows the signs of age and waning years. He has placed his hands upon the robust young son who is patient and attentive to the admonitions and prophecy of one whose end draws near.

The words Lehi spoke have been recorded in Second Nephi in the Book of Mormon. Among other things, he says that Joseph's seed shall not be destroyed and that there shall rise up one mighty among them who shall do much good, both in word and in deed. This monument is appropriate for the Hawaiian temple, since the Latter-day Saint Church has maintained a belief that Polynesians are descended of people spoken of in the Book of Mormon.

Lehi Blessing Joseph

HAWAIIAN MOTHERHOOD

As one approaches the temple itself, he mounts a few steps and passes a series of reflecting pools. At the head of the uppermost pool, slightly recessed and framed by climbing vines, is a panel in bold relief representing motherhood. The main figure is a Hawaiian mother, holding a giant clam shell and pouring water over her children. This is symbolic of mothers pouring out their love, hope, and care to their most wonderful possession, their children. Much has been written about motherhood, but the sculptor has caught a mood and action beyond verbal description.

Hawaiian Motherhood

THE BAPTISMAL FONT OF THE
HAWAIIAN TEMPLE

The purpose of temples in The Church of Jesus Christ of Latter-day Saints is for performing particular sacred services. These include baptism for the dead, ordination and associated endowments in the priesthood, marriage ceremonies, and other sealing ordinances. Baptismal fonts in the temples are used exclusively for vicarious baptism for the dead. Scriptures indicate that this ordinance was performed in the early Christian Church. In the epistle to the Corinthians, Paul said, "Else what shall they do which are baptized for the dead, if the dead rise not at all, why are they then baptized for the dead?"

(I Corinthians 15: 29.)

This large font rests on the back of twelve oxen, symbolic of the twelve tribes of Israel. The other temples have a similar arrangement, while the baptismal fonts of ward and stake chapels used for the living are of simple design. It is noteworthy that the temple of Solomon in Jerusalem also had a great font supported by twelve oxen, with the same symbolism.

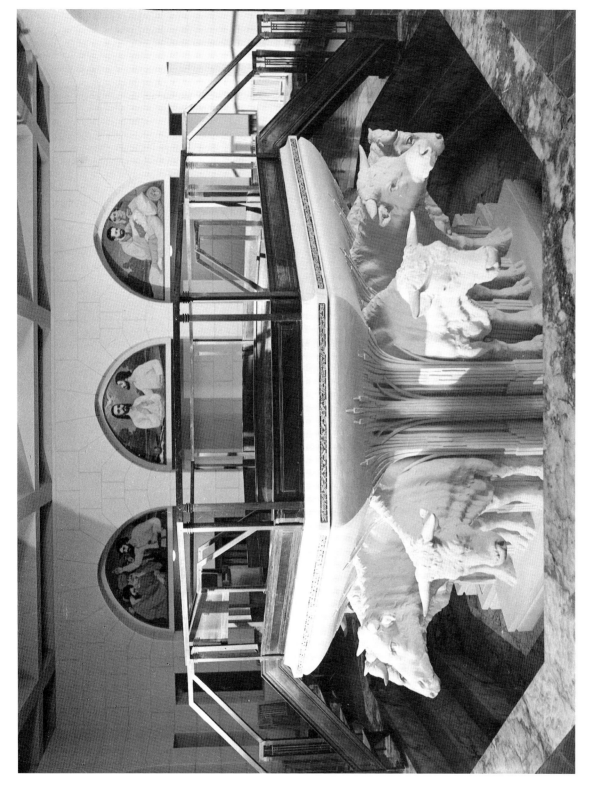

Baptismal Font of the Hawaiian Temple

The Church of Jesus Christ of Latter-day Saints

29

THE VISION

A youth in a frontier American village was troubled as to which sect to join during a movement of religious zeal that was storming the populace. His sincere and thoughtful soul was perplexed as ministers of several churches urged him to join their particular congregation. Even members of his own family were affiliated with different sects. After considerable discussion, investigation, and thought, he concluded that Bible study was the final recourse in which to find a solution to his problem. While reading in the Epistle of St. James, he was impressed by a passage in the first chapter, the fifth verse: "If any of you lack wisdom, let him ask of God, that giveth to all men liberally, and upbraideth not; and it shall be given him." This message seemed to strike him to the heart; here was a means for a solution to his bewilderment. With strong determination, early one morning he retired to the woods near his home in order to be alone. He had never before attempted a vocal prayer and began with considerable anxiety and hesitation.

The sculpture shows Joseph Smith kneeling, looking hopefully up into the heavens, at the moment prior to the manifestation of heavenly beings. There is an atmosphere of simplicity in his dress and frankness in his pose as he gazes upward seeking divine guidance. His serene humility attests the message of the sixth verse of the same chapter: "But let him ask in faith, nothing wavering. For he that wavereth is like a wave of the sea driven with the wind and tossed."

The Vision

JOSEPH SMITH THE PROPHET

The first study of Joseph Smith made by Avard Fairbanks was completed while he was still a youth in New York City. He had studied the facial features carefully from a death mask in possession of an artist he had met while studying sculpture. This sculptor, Louis Potter, had been loaned the original death masks of Joseph and Hyrum Smith in order that he could make portraits of them. These death masks were cast from molds of their faces made shortly after the martyrdom. The original death masks are protected in the archives in Salt Lake City. Later this sculptor took duplicate casts with him to New York City. With Mr. Potter's permission, Avard Fairbanks studied a set of copies. The mask of Hyrum had a large bullet wound above the nose to the left, and the cast even reproduced the blood clot present. Avard made twelve-inch diameter bas relief portraits of both Joseph and Hyrum Smith, hoping to make a number of sales when he returned to Utah; however, only a few were sold. Two copies were kept in the family and placed in the old homestead built by John Boyleston Fairbanks. Recently these have disappeared.

Avard Fairbanks has used his experience and knowledge of Joseph Smith's features many times since then for demonstration lectures. The sculptor has a phenomenal memory for facial features and details. He is able, after once having studied a great historical character, to model the person without reference to notes, photographs, or masks. More recently he has portrayed Joseph Smith in the following statues: "Joseph Smith's First Prayer," "Restoration of the Aaronic Priesthood," "Restoration of the Melchizedek Priesthood," and "Joseph Smith, the Prophet.

A study entitled "Joseph Smith with the Golden Plates" portrays this young man entrusted with the plates of the Book of Mormon. After a visitation by the Angel Moroni, Joseph Smith had gone to the Hill Cumorah near Palmyra, New York. At a location shown to him in a vision, he pried open a stone and

cement box which contained the plates. A heavenly messenger forbade him to touch them, but told him to return each year for instructions. On September 22, 1827, the fourth annual visit, Joseph Smith was allowed to take the plates for translation. He was charged with the responsibility of safekeeping for the plates. If he should let them go through carelessness or neglect, he would be cut off. All his endeavors were to be used to preserve and protect them until the messenger should again call for them.

During the translation, strenuous efforts were used to get the plates from Joseph Smith. Persecutions developed, and it became necessary for him to move to an adjacent state. There, in Susquehanna County, Pennsylvania, he met Oliver Cowdery, who agreed to be his scribe for the translation. Working together, the translation was completed and the Book of Mormon published.

While the Book of Mormon was being printed, Joseph Smith with five other men organized The Church of Jesus Christ of Latter-day Saints. The event was solemnized April 6, 1830, at the home of Peter Whitmer.

In another study, the sculptor portrays Joseph Smith as a sincere young man preaching the gospel, explaining the new evidences and revelations pertaining to the kingdom of heaven to an assembled group of saints, investigators, and curious townspeople. The stump of a tree serves as his outdoor podium. His right hand rests near the three books of sacred scripture, which include the Holy Bible, the Book of Mormon and the Pearl of Great Price. In his left hand are writings later to be assembled as the Doctrine and Covenants. He would speak in a low voice, not loudly, yet his words and ideas would captivate the audience. His pleasant and personable manner would make it appear as though he were speaking to each one individually. Although he had little schooling, he learned rapidly during his association with Oliver Cowdery,

Joseph Smith the Prophet, holding the Golden Plates

who was a teacher by profession. Joseph Smith traveled widely, preaching, admonishing Church members, and organizing new communities where he hoped the prejudices and persecutions would be infrequent. Many times the services of necessity were held out of doors, even in the cold weather. It is therefore historically correct for the artist to create a statue in an outdoor setting, with the Prophet shielded by his cape.

Joseph Smith was an extraordinary man, and was so considered by both his followers and his enemies. He was six feet tall and weighed about two hundred pounds. His chest and shoulders were broad. He participated and excelled in such athletics as wrestling, jumping, vaulting, and in pitching horseshoes, which was a popular sport in his time. His hair was auburn, much the same color as Brigham Young's. He was clean shaven and had his hair cut full, according to the custom of the times. His eyes were hazel and the lashes were long; his eyebrows were heavy. He was a commanding speaker with a low, soft voice. His manners were gentlemanly, he was personable and pleasant in spite of the opposition he encountered. In the twenty-four years following his first vision, he rose from obscure boyhood in a family with limited means to be the religious leader of twenty-five thousand people living at the frontier of a young nation. He had organized a church which had stirred considerable controversy, and his name was well-known throughout the land. He was reviled by his adversaries. He suffered trials and persecution. No less than thirty-eight times in fourteen years he was brought to court and yet was never convicted. Each time he would return to lead his people, admonishing them to forgive the oppressors (even though he had once spent six months in a dungeon), to live righteously, and to work productively. He planned and directed the building of cities and the erection of temples. He organized a militia and was mayor of Nauvoo, the city beautiful. Even a charter for a university had been requested. Unfortunately for his followers and for the state of Illinois, these plans, these efforts, and his life were suddenly terminated by assassins at the Carthage Jail.

Joseph Smith, portrait details

Joseph Smith the Prophet, proselyting among the people

JOSEPH SMITH, THE PROPHET

The Prophet is here depicted in an epic study in sculpture.

I have tried to portray him in the later years of his life as the stalwart person who brought to the world the messages of God for the guidance of the Saints of the Latter-Days.

In his left hand are held the books which are translations of the Book of Mormon and the Pearl of Great Price . In his right hand, along with the cape he holds other writings, at that time not yet compiled into book form. Therefore, they are shown as papers.

I have chosen to use a cape in this study. It gives to the entire composition a feeling of great dignity.

One part of the cape is slung back over his right shoulder. It flows around his right arm and renders an impressiveness to it. The length of this arm shows a long line down the side of the statue. In complement to this, on the opposite side and sweeping down from the bent arm, holding books, is another long line which renders a very beautiful draping of the cape. These two and other flowing lines have rhythmic harmonies.

Harmonies in sculptural forms are like the harmonies in music. If beautiful and well composed, we are drawn close to the spiritual harmonies of God through their contemplation.

The head of the statue is a part of the work in which I have taken a great deal of effort... To make the shape, form and facial likeness, I have used the death mask. However, construction alone is not sufficient. Through his face I have endeavored to portray the greatness of Joseph Smith, as a prophet; also that character who has gone through struggles and trying experiences and who possessed such great spirituality that God and Christ should choose him and place trust in him to usher forth the dispensation of the fullness of time.

Avard T. Fairbanks

Joseph Smith the Prophet, addressing the faithful

38

THE ANGEL MORONI

A colossal (three times life size) statue, cast in bronze and finished in gold leaf was placed on the top of the foremost spire of the magnificent six spired Latter-Day Saint Temple near Washington D.C. Subsequently Avard Fairbanks was requested to model a fifteen foot replica. A bronze cast finished in gold leaf was placed on the temple in Bellevue, Washington and additional copies were placed on the West Jordan Temple, the Denver Temple, and the Mexico City Temple.

As the first edition of this book was being printed, Avard Fairbanks was completing the colossal statue in Italy. He sent a letter about the progress a part of which is included.

Cara mia: (Dear ones)

Tonight I am writing from the quaint Italian city of Pietrasanta which is situated between Carrara and Pisa in the province of Tuscany. To the West is the Mediterranean Sea, and rising to the East is the Cararra range of the Appenine mountains. Marble carving and a bronze foundry are the major industries in this city of about 9,000 inhabitants.

Since the middle of winter I have been here working on the Angel Moroni statue which will be erected on a spire of the Washington D.C. temple. Presently, the figure is being enlarged from a six foot model to an 18 foot colossal statue, at the studio of the foundry where it will be cast in bronze. Because I must give instructions to the Italian artisans in their own language, I have had to review my knowledge of the language which I learned many years ago when we lived in Firenze (Florence) for a year. The chill of the Appenine winter is still with us. As the Europeans do not heat buildings as we do in the United States, it has been necessary to dress very warmly while working in the studio. Spring will be welcomed here. The work is progressing well, although the final bronze will not be completed until summer, nor shipped until August.

This statuary will memorialize the appearance of the Angel Moroni to Joseph Smith during the night of September 21, 1823. A description of this divine personage was written by the Prophet when he related the origin of the Book of Mormon.:

He had on a loose robe of most exquisite whiteness. It was a whiteness beyond anything earthly I had ever seen; nor do I believe that any earthly thing could be made to appear so exceedingly white and brilliant. His hands were naked, and his arms also, a little above the wrist; so, also, were his feet naked, as were his legs, a little above the ankles. His head and neck were also bare. I could discover that he had no other clothing on but this robe, as it was open, so that I could see into his bosom.

Not only was his robe exceedingly white, but his whole person was glorious beyond description, and his countenance truly like lightning. The room was exceedingly light, but not so very bright as immediately around his person. When I first looked upon him, I was afraid; but the fear soon left me.

(Pearl of Great Price, Joseph Smith 2:31-32.)

Dr. Fairbanks has this description in mind as he developed the figure of this heavenly personage. The figure and robe are magnificent, as described by the Prophet. The texture of the sculpture is made to scintillate in the light. The face is modeled from the artist's concept of ideal features, showing expressions of sincerity and benevolence and deep concern as he heralds the coming forth of a new dispensation on the earth in these latter days.

In Moroni's left arm he holds the golden plates from which the *Book of Mormon* was translated. His feet are just alighting on the orb that is symbolic of the earth to which he has come. It represents his return to the world to reveal to mankind further scriptures which he had hidden in the Hill Cumorah.

The sculptor conceives the angel as being weightless, his powers not being governed by earthly gravitational pull. Recent journeys by our astronauts between celestial spheres have presented to the sculptor the realization of the weightlessness of those in space. This representation of weightlessness testifies to the greatness of God's power and the immensity of his works, and of his creations in celestial time and space.

The trumpet held aloft in the right hand of the Angel Moroni portrays him as heralding the great events to come, including the restoration of the gospel in the latter days, as well as other visions and revelations which were to follow his appearance. The angel's coming fulfilled the prophecy of the Apostle John, as recorded by him in the Book of Revelation while on the Island of Patmos:

> And I saw another Angel fly in the midst of heaven, having the everlasting gospel to preach unto them that dwell on the earth, and to every nation, and kindred, and tongue, and people,

> Saying with a loud voice, Fear God, and give glory to him; for the hour of his judgment is come: and worship him that made heaven, and earth, and the sea, and the fountains of waters.

> Revelations: 14: 6-7.

The appearance of the Angel Moroni, and the subsequent translation of the Book of Mormon, initiated a new dispensation of God's inspired word to mankind. This concept is most appropriately set forth in the ninth *Article of Faith* of The Church of Jesus Christ of Latter-day Saints:

> We believe all that God has revealed, all that He does now reveal, and we believe that He will yet reveal many great and important things pertaining to the Kingdom of God.

A LETTER FROM PIETRASANTA

The following letter illustrates the sculptors love of Art and his desire to share his experiences, and his testimony of the Gospel of Jesus Christ with his family. He often traveled to Italy spending six weeks each trip modeling sculpture and finishing marble carvings.

Cara Mia: (Dear Family)   30 September 1973

I have come to Pietrasanta, Italy to finish some sculptures in clay, to be cast in bronze. One is a cougar, and another is Florence Nightingale. I think of Pietrasanta, a small community near the Italian Riviera, as the city of sacred stone, since that is its meaning in Italian. It was here that Michelangelo Buonarroti came centuries ago. The wealthy and powerful Medici family had a home or villa on the hill overlooking Pietrasanta, and Michelangelo signed some of his contracts there. It is therefore a city rich in historical significance.

The Carrara range was a source of marble even during the period of the Roman Empire. Quarrying resumed during the Renaissance. Michelangelo went up from this city, then a village, into the Carrara Mountains and discovered the site of the most choice stone for fine sculpture, and established a quarry. Pietrasanta has since become the city of artisans who carve the marble into beautiful statues for churches, gardens, and museums all over the world.

Marble is quarried in much the same fashion as in the days of Michelangelo, but it is now modified with power tools. One might suppose that there is a clear strata of pure white glistening stone. In reality, the marble is streaked with gray, and many blocks are quarried, (about a hundred) for every five blocks of choice marble. The gullies and canyons below the quarries appear white, as though laden with snow, with the discarded chips and blocks of imperfect stone.

Fine marble blocks are brought down to the studios in the city where work progresses fairly rapidly; subjects of all kinds take form. By the deft wielding of hammer, chisel, and pneumatic carving tools, portraits, saints and angels emerge from the shapeless, dazzling white, inanimate stone, which has lain dormant for millennia in the mountain crags.

I have come here to complete my sculpture and carve in marble. Even though the artisans are very skilled, I must always finish the carving to accentuate the details, and add expression to the features.

Here in the studios where I often work are models of sculpture in gesso, (Italian term for plaster), which are available to be duplicated in marble. They are in many categories: antiques, Greek, Roman, Renaissance, fountain and fantasy subjects, crucifixes, madonnas, and many others.

Statue of the Angel Moroni

Among the many other figures we find old testament prophets, patriarchs, apostles, and the christian angels. Most impressive are the portrayals of Jesus Christ. Numerous models of these subjects are to be found in the many marble carving studios. The workers here appear to thrive on artistic creation. They deeply appreciate the opportunity to work on new masterpieces of sculpture.

At the time I came to Pietrasanta, the enlargers were finishing a study of Mercury, originally made during the high renaissance by John of Bologna. It was an enlargement of his study. Presently, there is a copy in bronze of this same work as a central figure in the National Museum in Washington D.C. Mercury, in Roman Mythology (Hermes in Greek Mythology), was the messenger of the Gods.

Other projects have involved the casting of heroic monuments in bronze, since here there are also fine bronze foundries. When I was commissioned to create the colossal sculpture of Angel Moroni, eighteen feet tall, previous experience assured me that the work could be enlarged and cast in bronze here with the finest craftsmanship.

Therefore, it was to Pietrasanta that I came with a new creation to be made of another angel from on high. The Angel Moroni statue, one to be placed on a high spire of the beautiful new and awe inspiring Latter-Day Saint Temple under construction in Washington D.C. This angel is to be finished in gold leaf, a colossal statue and a colossal concept, one of the greatest ever.

The Angel Moroni is a messenger from God the eternal Deity, who is our creator and grants man life eternal. With the trumpet (clarion), Angel Moroni is the Herald to announce the glorious events which have and will come to pass here on earth in the last days. These include the Restoration of the Aaronic Priesthood, the Restoration of the Melchizedek Priesthood, the Restoration of the Church of Jesus Christ in these Latter-Days, and the Restoration of the Keys of Endowments in the Temples of the Lord by Elijah, the Prophet. The vision in which Angel Moroni appeared recalls the first vision of the prophet in which God the Father and the Son, Jesus Christ appeared to Joseph Smith. Here in the same studio, a life size marble of His First Vision was completed several years ago. Both commemorate events in the Latter-Day Restoration of the fullness of the Gospel and its establishment for the benefit of Mankind in the Plan of Salvation.

I am tired from long hours of the busy days work, and have only been able to briefly write a few of my thoughts. Italy is a land of people, of history, of art, of traditions and many other facets of human endeavor. It is a very interesting culture, and yet different than what we are accustomed to in the western United States.

Today, as I was working, I watched from the window the children passing by on the way to school. They are dressed in their grimbulies, (the black tunic with two accent stripes about the collar and down the right side, the colors designating which class the student belongs). It is reminiscent of the times our children attended one year of school in Firenze (Florence), Italy. The nostalgic image comes back very vividly from those days in 1928.

The work will be finished and I will be leaving Italy again very soon. My thoughts turn again to the family. Please convey my love in abundance to all.

Father

Colossal Bronze Statue of Angel Moroni,
which was placed on a spire of the Washington D.C. Temple

43

MONUMENT TO THE THREE WITNESSES TO THE BOOK OF MORMON

As the translation of the Book of Mormon by Joseph Smith from ancient plates of gold inscribed with curious characters neared completion in 1829, he was commanded to show the plates to three trusted associates who had assisted during this work. Oliver Cowdery, David Whitmer, and Martin Harris, in the presence of an heavenly angel, were permitted to view the record. They wrote out a testimony, and each signed it as a verification that these plates were real. There had been considerable skepticism, as the translation had been done in secret, according to commandment.

This monument, on Temple Square in Salt Lake City, portrays in bas relief the heads of Oliver Cowdery, David Whitmer, and Martin Harris. Below this is a copy of their testimony.

Be it known unto all nations, kindred, tongues, and people, unto whom this work shall come: That we, through the grace of God the Father, and our Lord Jesus Christ, have seen the plates which contain this record, which is a record of the people of Nephi, and also of the Lamanites, their brethren, and also of the people of Jared, who came from the town of which hath been spoken. And we also know that they have been translated by the gift and power of God, for his voice hath declared it unto us; wherefore we know of a surety that the work is true. And we also testify that we have seen the engravings which are upon the plates; and they have been shown unto us by the power of God, and not of man. And we declare with words of soberness, that an angel of God came down from heaven, and he brought and laid before our eyes, that we beheld and saw the plates, and the engravings thereon; and we know that it is by the grace of God the Father, and our Lord Jesus Christ, that we beheld and

bear record that these things are true. And it is marvelous in our eyes. Nevertheless, the voice of the Lord commanded us that we should bear record of it; wherefore, to be obedient unto the commandments of God, we bear testimony of these things. And we know that if we are faithful in Christ, we shall rid our garments of the blood of all men, and be found spotless before the judgment-seat of Christ, and shall dwell with him eternally in the heavens. And the honor be to the Father, and to the Son, and to the Holy Ghost, which is one God. Amen

> Oliver Cowdery
> David Whitmer
> Martin Harris

On the reverse side in bas relief is a plaque representing St. John, in exile on the Isle of Patmos, receiving his revelations. One arm is outstretched. The right hand shades his eyes as he appears to be gazing into the distant sky. He seems to be saying:

"And I saw another angel fly in the midst of heaven, having the everlasting gospel to preach unto them that dwell on the earth, and to every nation, and kindred, and tongue, and people, Saying with a loud voice, Fear God, and give glory to him; for the hour of his judgment is come: and worship him that made heaven, and earth, and the sea, and the fountains of waters."   (Revelation 14:6-7.)

This revelation was fulfilled by the Angel Moroni delivering the golden plates to Joseph Smith, and the subsequent translation, printing, and distribution of the Book of Mormon.

Monument to the Three Witnesses, west view

Monument to the Three Witnesses, east view

David Whitmer

Oliver Cowdery

Martin Harris

47

THE REVELATION
of
SAINT JOHN
THE DIVINE

CHAPTER XIV
Verses VI-VII

And I saw another angel fly in the midst of heaven, having the everlasting gospel to preach unto them that dwell on the earth, and to every nation, and kindred, and tongue, and people.

Saying with a loud voice, Fear God, and give glory to him; for the hour of his judgment is come: and worship him that made heaven, and earth, and the sea, and the fountains of water.

The Revelation of St. John the Divine

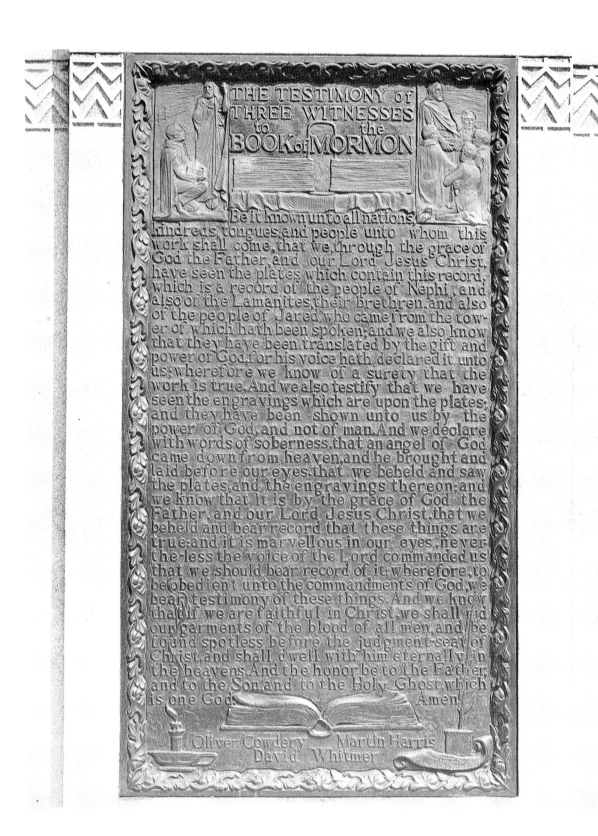

The Testimony of the Three Witnesses

49

RESTORATION OF THE AARONIC PRIESTHOOD

While Joseph Smith was translating the Book of Mormon , with Oliver Cowdery's assistance as scribe, in May of 1829 they retired to the woods to pray. Their purpose was to inquire of the Lord respecting baptism for the remission of sins, which they had found mentioned in the translation of the plates. While they were praying a messenger from heaven descended in a cloud of light, laid a hand on each of the two young men and ordained them saying:

Upon you my fellow servants, in the name of Messiah I confer the Priesthood of Aaron, which holds the keys of the ministering of angels, and of the gospel of repentance, and of baptism by immersion for the remission of sins; and this shall never be taken again from the earth, until the sons of Levi do offer again an offering unto the Lord in righteousness.

Doctrine and Covenance 13

This heavenly being identified himself as John, "the same that is called John the Baptist." He informed them he was acting under the direction and authority of Peter, James, and John, the ancient Apostles. He commanded them to go to the river to baptize, and ordain one another.

It was appropriate that John the Baptist should have been sent to confer and restore the Aaronic Priesthood, for it was written in the gospel of Luke that disciples of John the Baptist had come to Christ and asked:

Art thou he that should come? or look we for another?

Then Jesus answering said unto them, Go your way and tell John what things ye have seen and heard.

And blessed is he, whosoever shall not be offended in me. And when the messengers of John were departed, he began to speak unto the people concerning John, What went ye out into the wilderness for to see? A reed shaken with the wind?

But what ye went out for to see? A prophet? Yea, I say unto you, and much more than a prophet.

This is he, of whom it is written, Behold, I send my messenger before thy face, which shall prepare thy way before thee.

For I say unto you, Among those that are born of women there is not a greater prophet than John the Baptist:

Luke 7:20-28

This monument was erected on the temple grounds just north of the Tabernacle, but has since been moved to the east wall of Temple Square. It commemorates the Restoration of the Priesthood of Aaron, which had been lost from the earth for many hundreds of years through ignorance, iniquity and political corruption of the Savior's Church. The sculpture, which is heroic in proportions, is cast in bronze and mounted on a granite pedestal.

Another commemorative monument to the Restoration of the Aaronic Priesthood was created by Dr. Fairbanks in bold relief with life size figures. It was cast in bronze and mounted on a carnelian granite pedestal and shaft, quarried at Cold Springs, Minnesota. The memorial was erected and dedicated in Harmony, Susquannah County, Pennsylvania. It stands on the banks of the Susquahanna River at approximately the baptismal site, as well as can be determined, and near the house where Joseph Smith translated the Book of Mormon.

Justin Fairbanks assisted his father with both monuments.

Restoration of the Aaronic Priesthood

John the Baptist, modeled by the sculptor

Commemorative Panel Erected at Harmony, Pennsylvania

RESTORATION OF THE MELCHIZEDEK PRIESTHOOD

The priesthood of Melchizedek is first mentioned in Holy Scripture in the Book of Genesis when Abram returned victorious from the battle of the wicked kings.

And Melchizedek king of Salem brought forth bread and wine: and he was the priest of the most high God. And he blessed him, and said, Blessed be Abram of the most high God, possessor of heaven and earth.

Genesis 14:18-19

The priesthood of Melchizedek is again mentioned in a psalm of David:

The Lord hath sworn, and will not repent, Thou art a priest for ever after the order of Melchizedek.

Psalms 110:4

In his epistle to the Hebrews, the apostle Paul refers to these ancient scriptures as a prophecy of Jesus Christ.

So also Christ glorified not himself to be made an high priest; but he that said unto him, Thou art my Son, today have I begotten thee. As he saith also in another place, Thou art a priest forever after the order of Melchizedek. Though he were a Son, yet he learned obedience by the things which he suffered; And being made perfect, he became the author of eternal salvation unto all them that obey him; Called of God an high priest after the order of Melchizedek.

Hebrews 5:5-10

The Melchizedek Priesthood was restored to men on earth by a heavenly manifestation to Joseph Smith and Oliver Cowdery in the wilderness between Harmony and Colesville Pennsylvania, on the banks of the Susquahanna River. The exact date has not been determined, but according to The History of the Church it is thought to be in May or June of 1829. Reference was later made in the Doctrine and Covenance to this momentous event.

And again, what do we hear? The voice of Peter, James, and John in the wilderness between Harmony, Susquehanna county, and Colesville, Broome county, on the Susquehanna river, declaring themselves as possessing the keys of the kingdom, and of the dispensation of the fullness of times!

Doctrine and Covenants 128:20

Peter, James, and John appeared and ordained the two young men to the higher priesthood, bestowing on them the keys of apostleship which these three heavenly messengers held and had exercised in the former gospel dispensation. While the Aaronic Priesthood holds authority for the temporal affairs of the Church, the higher priesthood deals with spiritual matters. Consequently, all of the authority and power necessary for the establishment and development of the Church in the latter-days were restored to mortal men by this visitation.

Avard Fairbanks' monumental masterpiece, "The Restoration of the Melchizedek Priesthood", already cast in bronze, is a companion piece to the "Restoration of the Aaronic Priesthood". It was created to be placed on Temple Square in Salt Lake City. The artists conception reveals Joseph Smith, kneeling at prayer, receiving ordination, attended by Oliver Cowdery who is shown with head bowed. Three heavenly figures, Peter, James, and John are portrayed, standing above and conferring the Melchizedek Priesthood by the laying on of hands.

Justin Fairbanks assisted his father with this statue.

Restoration of the Melchizedek Priesthood

Among the memorabilia of the sculptor was found a letter by Avard Fairbanks announcing completion of casting of the monument.

July 19, 1972
The First Presidency
The Church of Jesus Christ
of Latter-Day Saints
Salt Lake City, Utah

Dear Brethren:

The Restoration of the Melchizedek Priesthood monument is now cast in bronze, and is awaiting instructions for shipment.

This heroic group in sculpture will be one of the worlds great masterpieces of our civilization. There are five figures in the composition. The three above portray Peter, James, and John - heavenly personages who came to Earth to confer the higher priesthood upon Joseph Smith and Oliver Cowdery. This monument will become to our day and period of cultural advancement, of importance in signalizing the: Age of the Restoration

And I am sure it will be of more significance than the portrayal of the four earthly figures of the Reformers, which famous heroic size memorial is erected in Geneva, Switzerland to the: Age of the Reformation

Having to teach the golden ages of cultures in the various Universities of America, truly I am grateful to have been commissioned to do the monuments to the Restorations of the two Priesthoods. I have been most earnest and prayerful in creating companion compositions and to utilizing of technical skills to be in harmony with the great subjects: "The Restoration of the Aaronic Priesthood" and "The Restoration of the Melchizedek Priesthood."

Also I do appreciate the opportunity to do the Angel Moroni for the Washington Temple.

It may be of interest to know that I have been made a "Socio" or member of the Society of Fine Arts of Florence, Italy - A venerable organization of great standing whose headquarters are in the "Casa di Dante" the home of Dante in Florence. This recognition places one in the forefront of Europe's most prominent men of cultural achievements.

May I take the occasion, at this time to express my sympathies in the loss of our Prophet, Joseph Fielding Smith and to tell of the confidence which I feel our people have in our new Prophet, Pres. Harold B. Lee and attending personnel of the First Presidency.

Your leadership will assure advancement and divine guidance in the work of the Lord.

Faithfully your brother
Avard T. Faribanks

The Apostle James, portrait

The Apostle Peter, potrait

The Apostle John, portrait

57

COMMEMORATIVE MEDALS
HONORING JOSEPH SMITH

At the request of the Heritage Mint Avard Fairbanks created six medals honoring Joseph Smith, the Prophet, portraying significant events in his life. Altogether he modeled twelve fifteen inch diameter bas reliefs medallions; six were modeled for the obverse and six for the reverse sides. These were cast in plaster, and from these casts dyes were cut. A series of six silver dollar size medals were then struck in either silver or bronze by the Heritage Mint. Bronze or silver blanks were heated to incandescence and squeezed between the dyes in great presses to produce these medals.

The obverse of the first medal, THE VISION, portrays Joseph Smith as a bewildered young man of fourteen studying the Bible, trying to find an answer as to which church he should join. There was considerable religious turmoil on the American frontier during Joseph Smith' youth, and several zealous ministers

each sought to have him join their congregation. Joseph did not know which was right, or which he should join. Seeking an answer to his questions in the scriptures, he was impressed with a passage in first chapter of the Epistle of James.

If any of you lack wisdom, let him ask of God, that giveth to all men liberally, and upbraideth not; and it shall be given him.

But let him ask in faith, nothing wavering. For he that wavereth is like a wave of the sea driven with the wind and tossed. James 1:5-6

The reverse of the medal portrays Joseph Smith in prayer in a secluded area of the woods near his family farm. Here, in answer to his first vocal prayer, two heavenly beings, in light and glory beyond comprehension, appeared. One addressed him by name and said, "This is My Beloved Son. Hear Him!"

(Joseph Smith - History 1:17).

The reverse depicts Joseph Smith apprehensively descending the Hill Cumorah after receiving the plates of gold. He has been warned that many would try to steal them. In the background, are the North and South American Continents, where those who made the records lived.

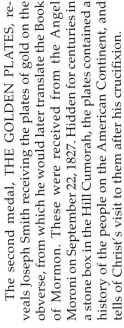

The second medal, THE GOLDEN PLATES, reveals Joseph Smith receiving the plates of gold on the obverse, from which he would later translate the Book of Mormon. These were received from the Angel Moroni on September 22, 1827. Hidden for centuries in a stone box in the Hill Cumorah, the plates contained a history of the people on the American Continent, and tells of Christ's visit to them after his crucifixion.

On the reverse is depicted the baptism of Joseph and Oliver. After conferring the Priesthood, John the Baptist then "...commanded us (Joseph and Oliver) to go and be baptized, and gave us directions..." Accordingly, they went into the Susquehanna River, where Joseph baptized Oliver first, and afterward Oliver baptized Joseph (Joseph Smith - History 1:70-71).

The third medal represents THE RESTORATION OF THE AARONIC PRIESTHOOD, May 15, 1829. John the Baptist, the same that baptized Jesus Christ, with his right hand on the head of Joseph Smith and his left hand on Oliver Cowdery, confers upon them the Aaronic Priesthood. This priesthood holds the keys and the authority to baptize in the name of Jesus Christ.

60

The fourth medal, representing THE RESTORA-TION OF THE MELCHIZEDEK PRIESTHOOD, shows Peter, James and John, original Apostles of Jesus Christ, conferring the Holy Priesthood by the laying on of hands.

When the Church of Jesus Christ of Latter-Day Saints was organized on April 6, 1830, Joseph Smith and Oliver Cowdery confirmed Hyrum Smith, Samuel H. Smith, David Whitmer and Peter Whitmer, Jr. as the first members of the church. The reverse of the Melchizedek Priesthood medal shows Joseph Smith, (center) and Oliver Cowdery confirming Hyrum Smith. In the background, left to right, stand Samuel H. Smith, David Whitmer, and Peter Whitmer, Jr.

On the reverse Joseph Smith is shown as the Prophet, Seer and Revelator, and the First President of the Church of Jesus Christ of Latter-Day Saints. In the background is the Nauvoo Temple. On the podium rests the Standard Works of the Church, which he held in his arm on the obverse. As he exhorts the faithful, he holds in his hand the Articles of Faith.

The fifth medal, THE LATTER-DAY PROPHET, portrays a dynamic, fearless, inspired prophet of God. In his hand is the Holy Bible, the Book of Mormon, the Doctrine and Covenants, and The Pearl of Great Price. This relief portrait represents a life time study with frequent modelings of the prophet by the master sculptor.

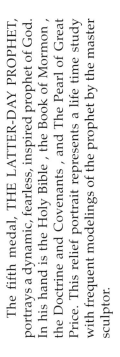

62

painted mob. "In life they were not divided, and in death they were not separated!" (Doctrine and Covenants 135:3). Each sealed his testimony with his blood.

The Jail at Carthage, Illinois is pictured on the reverse. The martyrdom of the Prophet, Joseph Smith and Hyrum, the Patriarch of the Church, did not prevent the Gospel from going forth in these Latter-days, nor stop God's holy work.

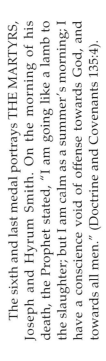

The sixth and last medal portrays THE MARTYRS, Joseph and Hyrum Smith. On the morning of his death, the Prophet stated, "I am going like a lamb to the slaughter; but I am calm as a summer's morning; I have a conscience void of offense towards God, and towards all men." (Doctrine and Covenants 135:4).

Both Joseph and Hyrum were shot in Carthage Jail about 5:00 P.M. on June 27, 1844 by an armed and

LEHI–NEPHI

The panel of Lehi and Nephi, modeled in bold relief, was erected at the side of the main entrance to the library at Brigham Young University. It represents the two most prominent figures in the first part of the Book of Mormon. The standing figure is Lehi holding the Liahona, a brass sphere of "curious workmanship" with two spindles, one of which directed Lehi and his followers in their journey to the Western Hemisphere. Nephi, his dutiful son, kneels as he holds two records. One record is a political history recording events of rulers and wars, and the other is of the ministry and of sacred writings. He is shown inscribing plates as his father relates a vision in which he saw the tree of life and a rod of iron leading to the tree. In the dream, a river of filthiness lies beyond the tree, and on the opposite bank are many people and a great building. These people mocked and scorned those who partook of the fruit of the tree of life. Some were ashamed and strayed from the tree into forbidden paths and were lost. This is one of the great and significant visions descried in the Book of Mormon. The lettering and the tree are stylized in the manner of ancient Central American decorative design.

Lehi-Nephi, relief panel at Brigham Young University Library

MORMON–MORONI

The panel of Mormon and Moroni, a companion piece to the Lehi and Nephi panel, is erected by the side of the main, entrance to the library at Brigham Young University. It represents the two most prominent personalities at the close of the Book of Mormon. Many ancient records had been collected by Mormon, and he had compiled an abridgement of many of these scriptures. Mormon is portrayed entrusting this record to his son Moroni. This abridgement, the Book of Mormon, was inscribed on plates of gold held together by rings. Besides being an historian, Mormon was also the religious and military leader of his people. He is therefore in a warrior's dress, with breastplate and helmet. On the breastplate, the sun is symbolic of eternal life and the celestial degree of glory, while the three vertical bars symbolize the three members of the Godhead. In the background is the Hill Cumorah, where the records were concealed by Moroni. Similar to the companion piece, the trees and the lettering are conventionalized to correspond to the style of ancient Central American decorative design.

Mormon-Moroni, relief panel at Brigham Young University Library

MORTAL MORONI

Following the last great battle between the Nephites and the Lamanites at Cumorah, Moroni alone of all the Nephites remained to finish the writings of his father and complete the record of his people. During this time, Moroni was a fugitive. Fearing destruction by the Lamanites, he wandered wherever he could for his safety. Eventually, he finished the record and hid the plates in the Hill Cumorah.

Avard Fairbanks heroic statue in bronze portrays Moroni as a mortal, wandering, clothed in animal skins and a cape, subsisting as best he could off the land. The records he had faithfully protected and completed he carries in his hand.

The erection of this monument on the grounds of the Manti Temple was especially appropriate since President Brigham Young pointed out that Moroni had dedicated this piece of land as a temple site many centuries before. There is a hill north of Manti which was found to have stratifications of Oolite, a type of sandstone. A quarry had been developed on the Northeast slope of this hill. Many buildings, including the Manti temple, have been constructed of this beautiful and durable, creamy white stone. At a conference in Ephriam, Sanpete County, Utah, where a discussion was held regarding possible temple sites, the consensus of opinion indicated that the quarry hill of Manti was the preferred site.

According to Orson F. Whitney in his book, The Life of Heber C. Kimball , President Brigham Young concurred, stating, "The Temple should be built on the Manti stone quarry." Later Brigham Young asked Warren Snow to accompany him to the hill in Manti where the Temple was to be erected. At the Southeast corner, Brigham Young said," Here is the spot where the prophet Moroni stood and dedicated this piece of land for a Temple site." The first Temple completed in what was then the Western Territories was the Manti Temple. It has served the temple needs of many people, and primarily those of Sanpete Valley, for many decades.

Mortal Moroni

MOSES DESCENDING
FROM MOUNT SINAI

After the children of Israel had fled from the oppression of Egypt, Moses led them to the desert lands near Mount Sinai. He had already declared unto the people the Ten Commandments revealed to him, but he went up again into the mountain for many days to commune with the Lord. However, Moses was on the mountain longer than the people expected and they began to lose faith. They urged Aaron, who was designated the leader in Moses' absence, to fashion a molten image, a golden calf, which he did. He placed it on an altar, around which the people made burnt offerings, feasted, and danced.

Meanwhile, Moses had nearly finished communing with the Lord.

"And he gave unto Moses, when he had made an end of communing with him upon Mount Sinai, two tables of testimony, tables of stone, written with the finger of God." (Exodus 31:18.) "And the Lord said unto Moses, Go, get thee down; for thy people . . . have corrupted themselves: They have turned aside quickly out of the way which I commanded them: . . . Now therefore let me alone, that my wrath may wax hot against them, and that I may consume them: . . . And Moses besought the Lord his God, and said Lord, why doth thy wrath wax hot against thy people?" (Exodus 32: 7-11.) He asked that his people be spared, reminding him of his promise to Abraham, Isaac, and Israel. "I will multiply your seed as the stars of heaven, and all this land . . . they shall inherit it forever." (Exodus 32:13.) Moses pleads: "Turn from thy fierce wrath, and repent of this evil against thy people." (Exodus 32:12.)

"And Moses turned, and went down from the mount, and the two tables of testimony were in his hand." (Exodus 32:15.) "As soon as he came nigh into the camp, that he saw the calf, and the dancing: and Moses' anger waxed hot, and he cast the tables out of his hands, and brake them beneath the mount." (Exodus 32 :19.)

The sculptor has caught the moment as he descends, staff in one hand, tables in the other. A justifiable anger pervades his whole being when he sees how quickly the children of Israel have reverted to idolatry.

Moses Descending from Mount Sinai

Moses Descending from Mount Sinai

Moses, Leader of the Ancient Exodus

72

Brigham Young, Leader of the Latter-day Exodus

73

ERECTED·IN·HONOR·OF
BRIGHAM·YOUNG
IN·COMMEMORATION·OF
THE·OUTSTANDING·SERVICE
HE·RENDERED·THE·INTER-
MOUNTAIN·WEST·AS·PATRIOT
PIONEER·COLONIZER·CHURCH
LEADER·AND·STATESMAN
ON·THIS·PLOT·OF·GROUND
AUG·19TH·1877·HE·DELIVERED
HIS·LAST·PUBLIC·ADDRESS
WHEN·HE·ORGANIZED·THE
BOX-ELDER·STAKE

Brigham Young Memorial at Brigham City, Utah
by J. Leo Fairbanks

74

ELIJAH, THE PROPHET, A SKETCH

I SHALL SEND YOU
ELIJAH THE PROPHET

Behold, I will send you Elijah the prophet before the coming of the great and dreadful day of the Lord:

And he shall turn the heart of the fathers to the children, and the heart of the children to their fathers, lest I come and smite the earth with a curse.
Malachi, 4: 5-6.

Elijah was one of the most important prophets in the Old Testament, and is often referred to in the New Testament. The First Book of Kings tells of miracles performed through Elijah's steadfast faith in The Lord. King Ahab and Queen Jezebel, who with their priests worshiped the Philistine diety, Baal, tried in vain to destroy Elijah, but he defied them. The Second book of Kings tells that he did not suffer death, but was taken up into heaven in a whirlwind by a chariot and horses of fire.

This same Elijah (or in the Greek, Elias) appeared with Moses before the apostles, Peter, James and John, to counsel with the Savior on the Mount of Transfiguration, as recorded in Matthew 17. The purpose of this visitation has remained a mystery to most of the Christian world. To the Latter-day Saints, however, its purpose is made clear in the revelation known as section 110 of the Doctrine and Covenants , of the Latter-day Saints Church wherein the Priesthood keys for the Gathering of Israel, committed by the Lord to Moses at the time of the Transfiguration, and the keys of Eternal Ordinances, committed to Elijah, were conferred upon Joseph Smith for the establishment of the Lord's Church on the Earth. These sealing keys which the artist has portrayed symbolically in the hands of this great prophet, are also referred to in Section 27 of The Doctrine and Covenants. The attitude of Elijah in this sketch, boldly holding and protecting the keys committed to his care, reflects the character of the Prophet as revealed in his life on Earth.

The following is a copy of a hand written letter, addressed to the leaders of the Church of Jesus Christ of Latter-day Saints, composed in a small room of the pension where the sculptor stayed during the time he worked on the monumental pieces in Italy, proposing a statue of the prophet he so greatly admired.

Pietrasanta, Italy   August 28, 1972

Dear Brethren:

While here in Italy, attending to final details and casting of the colossal Angel Moroni for the Washington D.C. Temple, I have had some opportunities to do some more carvings in marble. Such work has given me the inspiration for an heroic Elijah in this beautiful media of Cararra marble.

The last two verses in the Old Testament state the magnificent promise to the people here on Earth, so our beliefs and our Temple Endowments are ours because of the keys having been restored in the latter-days by Elijah.

My mind has continued to dwell upon the concepts of the worlds cultural periods in the history of civilization.

The Reformation was one in Europe; a great age of enlightenment.

Five hundred years ago in this area of the World, (Europe), a great intellectual awakening occurred. The Reformation was a very important period in the World's civilization; also called the age of discovery and the Renaissance. These occurred at he time of Columbus, Galileo, Copernicus, and also Michaelangelo.

Now, the Restoration is our Golden age. It must become the most important of all Times for it is The Fullness of Times.

Our creative Efforts in Art can be as outstanding as those of Donatello, Michaelangelo, Leonardo Da Vinci and other Renaissance artists who are so revered by the whole world.

There are now masterpieces which I have completed on subjects of the Restoration. One, carved in marble, is Joseph Smith and his (first) prayer.

These, cast in bronze in colossal or heroic size are:

The Angel Moroni with the Golden Plates, (another testament of Christ) colossal bronze.

The Restoration of the Aaronic Priesthood, heroic bronze.

The Restoration of the Melchizedek Priesthood, heroic bronze.

Now, (if I do not presume too much) I feel that an inspiration has come to me for the making of a great masterpiece of Elijah, the Prophet, which can become as impressive and outstanding and famous in the history of Art as the Moses by Michaelangelo. Elijah with the Keys, is a subject I feel I must do in a masterful Work of Art.

Among the great creations by masters of former cultural periods in Art, the subject of Elijah has not been made, because the Keys with which he was to come forth were not understood by leaders of the Christian Faiths, nor by the men of the Reformation.

When God and his Son Jesus Christ have brought forth through his prophets of today, the fullness of times and enlightenments to the minds of men; in many fields of intellectual endeavors as well as through the Gospel Plans.

The Restoration of the Keys in the Latter-Days by Elijah is of very great importance to the Fullness of the Gospel in the Fullness of Times, for they are the Restoration of the Temple Work and the ordinances and the endowments for the hereafter, and the fullness of man's glory, such are so well stated by words of God in the Pearl of Great Price:

"For behold, this is my work and my glory - to bring to pass the immortality and the eternal life of man."

Pearl of Great Price, Moses 1: 39.

Art plays a great part in every Golden Age of history. Therefore, today the arts which are sincere and are products of the most excellent techniques will evidence our spiritual importance in our Golden Age of the 20th Century.

A sketch of Elijah with the Keys I am sending on to you.

Sincerely your brother,

Avard T. Fairbanks

76

HARMONY AND MORALITY IN ART

Harmony may be considered as constructive and and orderly organization of forms (lines, masses, shapes, tones, colors, etc.) for the uplift and edification of man.

Destructive tendencies are the antitheses of the foregoing. Morality is a constructive order of life which leads to harmony in the Fine Art of Living.

To say that morality has nothing to do with art is a misstatement of the fundamental truths. It may be some persons' subjective rationalization and is often given out as aesthetic philosophy but as such has no basis in practical demonstrations.

Avard T. Fairbanks

LATTER-DAY SAINT EXHIBIT, CENTURY OF PROGRESS WORLD'S FAIR, CHICAGO, ILLINOIS, 1933-34

The display area in the Hall of Religion at this world's fair was partly historical and partly inspiration. While the large mural oil painting depicted events in LDS Church history, the sculpture complemented it by illustrating the ideals and philosophy of Mormon living. The central figure in bas relief is a young man in a loose flowing gown symbolically representing a heavenly being with arms outstretched giving this message to the people: "The glory of God is intelligence." Behind this figure may be seen rays which represent radiant energy constant in time and space. Below him is inscribed "Eternal Progress," a concept unique to Latter-day Saints that mortal life is a period in the spiritual existence of man, that he may progress through a series of steps after death and beyond resurrection. Eternal progress is here represented on the fundamentals of truth and love. The group to the right of the central figure represents the work of social groups, including the social worker with the basket of plenty ready to render services to the poor. This is symbolic of the Church Welfare Program and the women's Relief Society. The next group represents health, symbolic of the great importance of the physical body. Clean bodies are essential to clean minds. The Word of Wisdom was given and advocated for better health, for it is said, "The spirit of God will not dwell in unclean tabernacles." The scientist studying a reaction in the test tube symbolizes that truths of science are fundamentally a part of the completeness of knowledge. There cannot be a conflict between the facts of science and true religion. Next to the scientist is the teacher, spreading the knowledge of both science and religion. Beside him is a man holding the priesthood, either giving a blessing or ordaining by the laying on of hands by the power and authority of the priesthood. The man seated with his foot on the foundations of truth holds in his hands the books of revelation—the Bible, the Book of Mormon, the Doctrine and Covenants, and the Pearl of Great Price.

To the left of the central figure is the family. The father holds the baby, resting firmly on a foundation of love; the mother stands with her arm over the shoulder of her son, a Boy Scout. This all symbolizes the strong ties holding the family together, for marriage between Latter-day Saints is for time and eternity. The group of creative recreation is symbolic of the encouragement the Church gives to the expression of music, literature, drama, and the arts. Recreation and cultural development are fundamental and important aspects of overall progress of the individual.

The display was arranged with bas relief sculpture central and the murals extending around just above. At opposite ends of the exhibit were the life-size figures of "A Tragedy of Winter Quarters" and the sequel, "Youth and New Frontiers," one representing the struggle on the old frontier and the other, the opportunity in a new land and a new frontier of promise. Two stained glass windows designed by J. Leo Fairbanks were also exhibited. The first depicts Joseph Smith's first vision in the Sacred Grove. The other, titled "In Holy Temples," represents Elijah the prophet standing before the Salt Lake Temple. It was he who came to the Prophet Joseph Smith at the Kirtland Temple and restored the keys of salvation for the dead, thus fulfilling the prophecy of Malachi 4: 5-6:

> Behold, I will send you Elijah the prophet before the coming of the great and dreadful day of the Lord: And he shall turn the hearts of the fathers to the children, and the heart of the children to their fathers, lest I come and smite the earth with a curse.

The murals of great periods of Church history (not illustrated here) first show "Nauvoo the Beautiful," a prosperous Illinois city, followed by "Exodus from Nauvoo" across the ice of the Mississippi in the dead of winter. The Mormons are depicted as windswept and bleak as mob violence forced them to leave their homes. "Winter Quarters" was made in Florence, Nebraska, where many died. The "Pioneer Train on the March to the West," "The Encampment on the Plains," "The Mormon Battalion," "The Handcart Companies," and "The Pioneers Entering Salt Lake Valley," all depict the mass movement of thousands westward. The "First Winter in the Valley," and the "First Irrigation by Anglo-Saxons" reveal problems of the new settlers. Finally, a scene of prosperity, the "Desert Shall Blossom as a Rose," as seen from the steps of the University, shows accomplishment in spite of adversity. These murals were painted by John B. Fairbanks, the father, and J. Leo Fairbanks, the older brother. The painting and sculpture were designed to coordinate a story of history, philosophy, and motivation of The Church of Jesus Christ of Latter-day Saints.

Eternal Progress

79

THE TRAGEDY OF WINTER QUARTERS

The 1933 Chicago World Fair was a great success even though the nation was barely emerging from a severe depression. The Fair Commission decided to extend it for another year. The exhibit of the Church of Jesus Christ of Latter-Day Saints was so well received that arrangements for a larger space in the Hall of Religion was made. Avard Fairbanks offered to create two additional statues to augment the spiritual message, one of sorrow and one of hope.

Sketches were drawn and plans were submitted late in 1933 with the collaboration of President Romney of the Northern States Mission. With approval of the Latter-Day Saint Church authorities, modeling of the life size statues was begun in the spring of 1934, and rushed to completion. They were finished and delivered to Chicago just before the reopening of the World Fair.

The inspiration for the statue portraying the Tragedy of Winter Quarters dates back in pioneer history to a Fairbanks ancestor whose infant son was buried on the prairie. John Boylston Fairbanks and his wife, Sarah, also buried his father and her mother and father at the Winter Quarters Cemetery, during times of hardship, deprivation, and despair.

While visiting in Utah in the summer of 1931, Avard Fairbanks was requested to present a lecture to a meeting of the Daughters of the Utah Pioneers, which was convened at Brighton in Big Cottonwood Canyon. The concept of a grieving couple burying a child expresses the sorrow which too often was experienced by faithful pioneer parents. The demonstration lecture was very well received. During the presentation he explained the modeling of the figures and discussed pioneer history and philosophy. He gave several similar demonstration lectures that summer, and many influential persons were well impressed. After each lecture, the modeling was torn down and the clay was returned to a suitcase, but the concept continued.

During the family's return by automobile to Michigan, a special effort was made to visit the Winter Quarters Cemetery at Florence, Nebraska, (later incorporated into Omaha). Brigham Young's home was a historic site on a street bordering a park. Several people were asked where the cemetery was located, and they didn't know, but finally an older man directed the family to the location at the top of the hill. The cemetery was neglected and overgrown with weeds. The gate was rickety, and the fence was in disrepair. The cemetery had been used again by the community for several decades after the Mormons had moved to Utah, but was later partially abandoned. As the family looked about the cemetery, George Q. Cannon, a prominent person in the Latter-Day Saint Church had also come to visit the sacred place. In an ensuing conversation it was agreed that the neglect should be resolved and a suitable memorial erected.

This commemorative statue, The Tragedy of Winter Quarters, was first exhibited at the Hall of Religion at the Chicago World Fair in 1934. It reenacts moments of sorrow for many families who were forced to leave Nauvoo because of mob persecution in 1846. Many buried loved ones at Winter Quarters in Nebraska Territory, when disease, cold, and famine took a heavy toll of the very young and the old in the makeshift city of dugouts and sod shelters.

Here stand a young father and mother, pausing in a moment of silence over the open grave of their infant wrapped in a thin blanket. The father holds a shovel in one hand, while his broad cape protects his wife from the cruel wind. It may have been thus that John Boylston Fairbanks, the sculptor's grandfather, buried his first child, a son and namesake, in a small grave under the prairie sod. The composition is symbolic of the sorrow many other parents suffered who lost loved ones either at Winter Quarters or on the journey to the West.

A Tragedy of Winter Quarters

YOUTH AND NEW FRONTIERS

In sharp contrast to "A Tragedy of Winter Quarters," the companion statue portrays new life and hope. It was first displayed in the Latter-day Saint exhibit in the ,Hall of Religion at the Chicago World's Fair, a Century of Progress. "Youth and New Frontiers" depicts life, health, abundance through diligence, and a future to greet with enthusiasm. The man is placed characteristically as the foremost figure. He has to provide for the physical necessities of life. The mother is placed as the central figure and is upon a pedestal, an evidence of the high esteem in which Latter-day Saints hold womankind and especially mothers. There is an expression of purity and confidence as she gazes forward. The boy, with books in hand, is seeking other new frontiers, those of intellectual attainment. He stands ready to prepare himself to carry on the civilization we have today, as well as to advance it for tomorrow.

Although this statue was never cast in bronze, it is hoped that in the future its great message may be sufficiently appreciated that this masterpiece will be molded into a permanent material.

"New Frontiers" was featured on the cover of the Relief Society Magazine July, 1941. A description of the statue was printed on the inside cover, and deserves to be repeated.

The Pioneers faced a frontier which demanded struggle, sacrifice, and sorrow, but still they pressed on. Out in the West a culture charged with spirituality of mind, with plans for a splendid system of social organization, was fostered by the pioneer forefathers. Have the sons and daughters of these hardy people lost sight of the vision and foresight of their ancestors? We cannot falter, for today we have new frontiers to conquer.

The group of sculpture representing "New Frontiers," composed and placed in the Century of Progress Exposition in Chicago, was created to show that in our progress and development there are new frontiers for the descendents of the Pioneers.

In the arrangement of this particular group of sculpture, the mother is placed in an elevated position, symbolic of our American concept of the mother. She is the center about which the family life is grouped. She is honored, and it is her husband's desire to keep her thus. She seeks the refinements of life. She looks forward. She senses and feels the living development and the great future beyond. It is her duty to guide and direct the children toward futures of high purpose.

The courageous and strong husband provides the physical necessities of life. It may be noticed that in his right hand he grasps the vegetables and fruits of the fields, He cultivates or provides that which gives sustenance to his family. In his left hand he supports the child. It is the great responsibility of true manhood to sponsor, uphold and protect life.

The young boy at the opposite side of the group is shown with his books in his hand. He, as a symbol of youth, sees new fields of activity as a result of his learning. He is to carry on the culture of his progenitors.

As our religion's teachings point out that progress is eternal and that "the glory of God is intelligence," we must realize that we cannot come to the end of the horizon. It is constantly expanding and enlarging with our increased vision and activities.

This group of sculpture through its tranquility and its dignity manifests that the youth of today seeks to further advance the culture established by the great Pioneers. The youth of today also will take on the responsibilities of life. With force and energy it too will struggle and sacrifice and meet courageously its "New Frontiers."

Avard T. Fairbanks

Youth and New Frontiers

WINTER QUARTERS MONUMENT

The memorialization of Winter Quarters Cemetery at Florence, Nebraska, is more than a monument; it is an expression of a people that the sufferings of their pioneer ancestors were not in vain nor will they be forgotten. Since three of the sculptor's great-grandparents lie buried in this cemetery, one can understand the great pains he has taken to create a tribute for those who lie resting in the hallowed ground. Many others who helped plan and work with him toward the same goal have ancestors interred in the same cemetery. Together the sculptor, the stonecarver, and the landscape designer have achieved a deep feeling of awe and reverence for this sacred ground. It has become an important historical site, attracting thousands of visitors each year.

The walkway to the cemetery passes between two sandstone masonry pillars flanking the gate. Beautiful bronze panels are placed on these pillars, one symbolic of sorrow, the other of hope. The first has a figure clothed in a flowing robe, head bowed and partly covered by a loose hood. The inscription states: "Pioneer Mormon Cemetery" and "In loving memory of the six thousand devoted pioneers who died on the plains between 1846-1869. The bodies of nearly six hundred of those brave souls were buried within this sacred enclosure." The panel symbolizing hope is an inspired female figure looking upward, and the inscription states: "I am the resurrection and the life." "This mortal body is raised to an immortal body." (Alma 11:45.) "The dead shall hear the voice of the Son of God: and they that hear shall live." (John 5:25.) "For they shall rest from their labors here and shall continue their works." (Doctrine and Covenants 124: 86.)

Proceeding further up the path, one soon arrives at the monument centered in an amphitheater of shrubs and trees.

This great bronze statue of sorrowing parents was cast in heroic proportions and was erected in 1936 on the site of the Pioneer Mormon Cemetery. It is situated on a high hill commanding a view of Omaha and the Missouri River. It was placed on a pedestal cut from granite quarried in Little Cottonwood Canyon, the same granite used in the building of the Salt Lake Temple. Immediately around the monument is a sunken enclosure, or court, set off in Utah sandstone masonry. A few yards in front of the solemn figure is a great bronze panel nineteen feet wide on which are listed names of about four hundred of the known dead. In the center of the panel is the striking figure of a young man symbolic of the resurrection, stretching out his hands and giving the message: "Life is Eternal." Behind him are concentric radiant beams of the resurrected glory. These rays continue divergent from this figure between the pavement blocks of the court, crossed by concentric arcs. There are two areas where headstones of seven graves were found during the excavation. Spreading evergreen junipers were planted over the graves in place of concrete.

Immediately in front of the base of this monument, written in script, cast in bronze, and embedded in the pavement of the enclosure is a verse from the hymn, "Come, Come Ye Saints." "Gird up your loins, fresh courage take, our God will never us forsake." This hymn was written on the trek by William Clayton, who was inspired by deeds of heroism amid suffering and deprivations.

Seen from behind, the monument is also impressive. As the wind whips the father's cape, a low, scraggly, leafless bush fans out over the cape, giving the impression of a great gnarled skeleton hand, a hand of the cold, the wind, the snow, the deprivations, and the diseases, reaching out to grasp those who falter. There on the pedestal is a plaque depicting the wagon caravan on the trail to the West with the inscription:

Winter Quarters Memorial Marker

85

That the struggles, the sacrifices, and the sufferings of the faithful pioneers and the cause they represented shall never be forgotten, this monument is gratefully erected and dedicated by The Church of Jesus Christ of Latter-day Saints.

Of personal interest is a story told of my maternal great-grandmother, whose oldest child would not stay in the wagon unless he could see his mother's hand. While he was awake, she would walk alongside with her hand in the wagon box. On this plaque, to the observer's left, one sees a young woman walking beside the wagon in this manner.

Flanking a path around the edge of the sunken enclosure are embedded bronze plaques with inscriptions of poetic and scriptural phrases, reassuring us that their works continue and that death is but a step in the overall plan of eternal progression. The bronze plaques read as follows:

Rest for the weary soul
Rest for the aching head.
Rest on the hillside, rest
    With the great uncounted dead.
                    (Henry W. Naisbitt.)

They kept his commandments
    In life and in death.
        They were faithful
            In tribulation.
                (Doctrine and Covenants 58: 2 .)

For notwithstanding they die,
They also shall rise again,
A spiritual body.
                (Doctrine and Covenants 88: 2 7 .)

Come, come ye saints,
    No toil nor labor fear,
        But with joy
            Wend your way.
                        (William Clayton.)

O Lord, responsive to thy call.
In life or death what ever befall,
Our hopes for bliss on thee depend,
Thou art our everlasting friend.
                            (John Lyon.)

After much
Tribulation
Come the blessings.
                (Doctrine and Covenants 58: 4.)

Mourn not for those who peaceful lay
    Their wearied bodies down,
Who leave this frail and mortal clay
    To seek a fadeless crown.

Dry up the unavailing tear,
    Repress the selfish sigh;
Know that the spirit ransomed here
    Yet lives and never shall die.
                            (Edward Sloan.)

Because I live,
    ye shall live
        also.
                            (John 14 :19.)

For though from out our bourne of time
    And place—the flood may bear me far,
I hope to see my pilot face to face
    When I have crossed the bar.
                            (Alfred Tennyson.)

Behold, all things
    Have been done
In the wisdom of him
    Who knoweth all things.
                            (2 Nephi 2:24.)

Yea, and blessed are the dead
    That die in the Lord, . . .
        They shall rise from the dead
            And shall not die after.
                    (Doctrine and Covenants 63: 49.)

He that believeth on
    the Son
Hath everlasting life.
                            (John 3: 36.)

For I know that my redeemer liveth,
    And that he shall stand
        At the latter day
            Upon the earth.
                            (Job 19:25.)

If one should pause a moment and close his eyes, he might hear echoes returning out of the past, first a murmur, then a chant, and finally a chorus on the wind singing the last stanza of "Come, Come Ye Saints" bearing the courageous message: "But if our lives are spared again, To see the Saints, their rest obtain, O how we'll make this chorus swell—All is well ! All is well !"

One cannot leave this hallowed enclosure without a sense of reassurance that there is purpose to life, that death is not an end, and that the souls of those whose remains lie here have progressed into life eternal.

Pioneer Mormon Cemetery at Winter Quarters East Gate Entrance

"I am the resurrection and the life," companion entrance panel

Entrance panel, Pioneer Mormon Cemetery

89

Tragedy of Winter Quarters Monument in Sacred Enclosure
of the Pioneer Mormon Cemetery

THAT THE STRUGGLES THE SACRIFICE
THE SUFFERINGS OF THE FAITHFUL
AND THE CAUSE THEY REPRESENTE
NEVER BE FORGOTTEN THIS MON
GRATEFULLY ERECTED AND DE

CHURCH OF JESUS CH
FIRST PRESIDENCY: HEBER J
SCULPTOR: AVARD FAIRBANKS

A posterior view of Monument A Tragedy of Winter Quarters

91

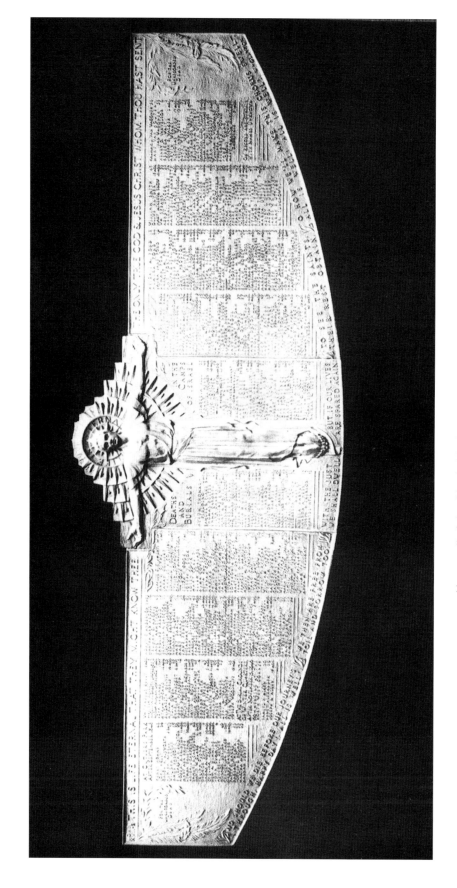

Honor roll of dead buried in the Winter Quarters cemetery

Central figure of Honor Roll panel

THAT THE STRUGGLES THE SACRIFICES AND
THE SUFFERINGS OF THE FAITHFUL PIONEERS
AND THE CAUSE THEY REPRESENTED
NEVER BE FORGOTTEN. THIS MONUMENT IS
GRATEFULLY ERECTED AND DEDICATED

BY THE
CHURCH OF JESUS CHRIST OF LATTER-DAY SAINTS
FIRST PRESIDENCY: HEBER J. GRANT. J. REUBEN CLARK, JR.. DAVID O. McKAY
SCULPTOR: AVARD FAIRBANKS (A DESCENDANT OF PIONEERS BURIED HERE)

Dedication panel on pedestal of Winter Quarters Monument

Winter Quarters Monument Dedication

The dedication of the monument honoring those who were buried at the cemetery was held on September 20, 1936. After a week of intermittent cloudy days with some light rain, the sky cleared and a beautiful clear day greeted the assembled participants. Many notables, including state and city officials as well as prominent Latter-Day Saint Church authorities, were in attendance. President Heber J. Grant gave the main address, and many others gave inspiring speeches.

A group photograph following the dedication included a large number of important and interested persons. Immediately in front of the statue is seen President Heber J. Grant. On his right is David O. McKay and on his left is George Albert Smith. Both later served as Presidents of the Latter-Day Saint Church. On the far left is Avard Fairbanks, Sculptor, and on the far right is an elderly gentleman with a goatee, John B. Fairbanks, the sculptor's father, who three years before had created many paintings for the World Fair exhibit in Chicago. He proudly joined in the ceremonies.

GOD BLESS OUR HOME

At dusk and the end of the day, a family pauses for a moment to communicate their thoughts of love and thanksgiving to the Lord. The circumstances are not special, although it could be to ask protection for an older son away form home on a mission or in the service of his country. Perhaps a son or daughter is away at school, away form the guiding influence of parents. However, isn't he or she still a part of the home? Thanks are given and blessings asked with deep sense of humility and reverence. Yes! Teach them to pray while they are yet in childhood and let all join in family prayer.

This statuette honors the love, hope, faith, and unity of the Latter-day Saint family.

God Bless Our Home

RELIEF SOCIETY CENTENNIAL MEMORIAL
INSCRIPTION OF PANEL

Here in the shadow of the temple, on this spot hallowed by the tread of pioneer feet, the Relief Society-woman's benevolent organization of The Church of Jesus Christ of Latter-day Saints erects this monument.

It stands as an expression of appreciation for the wondrous opportunities for soul growth that have come to womankind since the time one hundred years ago when, in 1842, the Relief Society was organized in Nauvoo, Illinois, by the Prophet Joseph Smith, who said: "I now turn the key in your behalf in the name of the Lord, and this society shall rejoice, and knowledge and intelligence shall flow down from this time henceforth; let kindness, charity and love crown your works."

In this tower hangs the famed Nauvoo Temple bell, whose life-time spans a century of Church history. A sentinel in the sacred temple at Nauvoo, the bell in vibrant tones rang out the changing moods of the faithful as they experienced first peace and joy, and later the anguish of parting from all that they had toiled to build. Immediately following the original pioneers, with Brigham Young at their head, came the second company in the great exodus to the West. Heading this veritable host of Israel, the bell played well its part in the westward trek. It awakened the herdsman at dawn, called the saints from their wagons to kneel in morning prayer, rang again to start the day's march, and in the solemn stretches of the night it quieted the fears of the people as it warned stray Indians that the sentry was at his post.

It is with gratitude that this monument is dedicated to the thousands of unsung Relief Society heroines who, over a period of one hundred years, have stimulated intellectual development and given compassionate service without thought of honor or reward. These valiant women have nourished the hungry, clothed the needy, nursed the sick, buoyed up the discouraged and disconsolate, and tenderly prepared the dead for burial.

Relief Society Presidents, 1842-1942:

Emma Smith	Emmeline B. Wells
Eliza R. Snow	Clarissa S. Williams
Zina D. H. Young	Louise Y. Robison
Bathsheba W. Smith	Amy Brown Lyman

Nauvoo Temple Bell Tower

THE RELIEF SOCIETY CENTENNIAL MEMORIAL
COMMEMORATIVE PANEL

This commemorative panel has an explanatory inscription telling of the early history of the Relief Society. In the background is portrayed a front view of the Nauvoo Temple prior to its destruction through fire set by mobs. In the lower corner, to the observer's right, is the sun sending great rays of light. It symbolizes the celestial degree of glory in the hereafter, which is often likened to the radiance of the sun. In the upper right corner is the moon, symbolizing the terrestrial degree of glory. As in the scriptures (Doctrine and Covenants 76), it is likened to the radiance of the moon. The telestial degree of glory, likened to stellar light, is represented by three stars. The number three is also representative of the fundamental plan of three, not only in the Godhead, but also in the leadership in all organizations of the Church. Sweeping from the right lower corner up to the observer's left are clouds enshrouding the base of the temple, symbolizing the creative powers of God in the great vastness of material substance. "And the Spirit of God moved upon the face of the waters." (Genesis 1: 2.) Arched above the clouds is the rainbow, a symbol of promise. It is a sign of God's promise to Noah that the earth would never again be completely engulfed in a deluge. Just below the moon is a nebula, a galaxy faintly seen in the background as a spiral of glimmering light, symbolic of the universe with its many galaxies. At the base of the panels to the observer's left is the seal of the Relief Society. This seal has an inscription, "Charity Never Faileth." (1 Corinthians 13:8.) The torch of enlightenment is at the base of the seal. An honor roll is in the lower center with the names of the presidents who had served since its establishment in 1842 until 1942 when the memorial panels were cast in bronze.

Relief Society Centennial Memorial

PIONEERING

This panel commemorates the capacity of the saints to overcome the adversity and struggles encountered in life. The scene is the crossing of the Mississippi River on solid ice from Nauvoo to Montrose, Iowa, a miracle comparable to the crossing of the Red Sea, for the Mississippi rarely freezes at that place. The background was taken from an old drawing of the exodus from Nauvoo as it was being deserted because of mob violence. Prominent on the skyline is the temple, soon to be engulfed in flames. In the foreground is a family group, demonstrating that pioneering was a hardship shared by the whole family. The wife and mother is the central figure because of her importance in conquering adversity. The stark and bare tree of winter attests to the severity of conditions. The wagon, symbolic of the home, is still the center of family activities, although it is but a makeshift one. The spinning wheel symbolizes industry, as the members of the Relief Society fulfilled an important function on the trek West. At the base, an inscription reads: "No toil nor labor fear." As they march forward into the future, the father bears in his arms a small infant who represents the new generation.

Panel honoring Pioneering

EDUCATION

The panel titled "Education" portrays the development of the mind. The standing figures in the background portray the great field of intellectual quests of science, arts, and religion. Science is represented by a young man in a laboratory coat standing near a microscope. Next to him is a young woman with a painter's palette, representing the arts. The dove is symbolic of the Spirit of the Holy Ghost. An older man dressed in ancient robes and holding scrolls, documents, history of laws, and prophecy, represents religion. His right arm reaches toward the youth as though he is saying: "Follow in the paths of truth and righteousness." In the center foreground is a teacher with an open book, teaching the young girl standing behind her. The girl gazes at a sphere, the world, and ponders what it holds; she is looking into the future. Behind the sphere and sweeping diagonally across the panel is a broad arc, symbolic of the orbit of the earth and the plane of the ecliptic on which the planets of the solar system revolve about the sun. It comes first past the ancient man and then on to the young scientist as if out of the past, through the present, and into the future. The seated figure is a mother who is holding four books: the Holy Bible, the Book of Mormon, the Doctrine and Covenants, and the Pearl of Great Price. She gazes upward to a dove, the sign of the Holy Ghost: education in the home needs the constant influence of the Holy Spirit. At the base of the panel are books signifying the importance of literature and recorded information; in the corner is the lamp, a symbol of education which gives light and knowledge. As one studies the panel, it becomes apparent that the scientist, the artist, the man of religion, and the mother all look toward the dove for inspiration through the Holy Spirit, an important factor in all endeavors. The inscription below states: "The glory of God is intelligence," a quotation from the Doctrine and Covenants 93:36. This profound concept motivates the unrelenting promotion of education by The Church of Jesus Christ of Latter-day Saints.

104

Panel representing Education

BENEVOLENCE

A panel titled "Benevolence" portrays the Relief Society as it exerts maternal guidance over all, from infancy to advanced age. The star in the center background is a symbol of the doctrine of love manifest when Christ came to earth to proclaim the principles of that doctrine. A youth looks to the star, seeking heavenly guidance just as the wise men of old sought the Lord by following the star of Bethlehem. The central figure is womanhood at the height of her capabilities, giving encouragement to the young mother, to the youth, and to the aged sister. The wheat in the background symbolizes the gathering of food for times of need. The figure to the observer's right represents a spirit of cooperation and actual material assistance supplied by the Relief Society work. With her right arm the woman steadies the elderly sister, rendering spiritual guidance. In her left arm she holds a basket of fruits and vegetables, indicating physical assistance to the point of self-help. The inscription at the base of the panel appropriately describes the benevolence of the Relief Society: "Through love serve one another."

Panel symbolizing Benevolence

107

MONUMENT TO THE FIRST SUNDAY SCHOOL

A monument commemorating the first Sunday School in Utah was erected at the corner of Third South and First West, Salt Lake City. It is a panel depicting Richard Ballantyne teaching several students in his pioneer home, for the moment converted into a classroom. The sculpture is cast in bronze and mounted on a hewn granite slab.

Richard Ballantyne, described as an early Mormon stalwart, was born in Whitridgebog, Scotland, in 1817. Because of his father's death, he was required to go to work at the age of eleven. He apprenticed as a baker; later he established his own business and prospered. He was active in the Presbyterian Church, serving as a Sunday School teacher to a class of seventy-five boys and girls. When missionaries visited his town of Earlston in 1839, he became very interested in their preaching. Shortly after he was baptized, he immigrated with his family to Nauvoo, Illinois, where he took an active part in Church work.

At one time, while harvesting wheat, he and five other men were waylaid and held as hostages. For fourteen days they were detained and were threatened several times with death, but they were released when Nauvoo officials dropped charges against two apprehended terrorists. When the Mormons left Nauvoo, Richard Ballantyne accompanied the main group to Council Bluffs, and to Winter Quarters in 1847. He and his family arrived in Salt Lake Valley in 1848. During the summer of 1849, he built an adobe home about one-half mile south and west of the temple block, and by winter it was ready for occupancy. One Sunday in December, 1849, he invited a group of thirty neighborhood children, ages three to thirteen, into his parlor, rearranged as a classroom, and led them in singing and gospel instruction. This home was the first Sunday School and it continued to serve as such until this class instruction was transferred to his ward chapel. In time, the value of Sunday School was recognized for the Church generally.

Many monuments have been erected to dramatic or tragic events of history, while other humble events with ultimately greater effect may often be overlooked and forgotten. It is duly appropriate that Richard Ballantyne's efforts be memorialized; indeed, he had the faith of a mustard seed, for he recognized that the future strength of the Church depends on instruction given its youth.

The inscription is a quotation from Richard Ballantyne.

"I knew that the gospel was too precious to myself to be withheld from the children. They ought to have the privilege of the gospel teaching, and that was the main purpose, to teach them the gospel."

The First Sunday School

109

THE PRIMARY CHILDREN'S HOSPITAL PANEL

This beautiful and impressive group, cast in ivorytoned epoxy resin, is situated at the main entrance to the Latter-day Saint Primary Children's Hospital in Salt Lake City, Utah. It is titled "Suffer Little Children to Come Unto Me, For They Are of the Kingdom of Heaven."

In the foreground a child stands, representing those who have been healed of their infirmities and restored to health through care in the hospital. Dressed in a hospital robe, he clasps a sphere. One might assume it is a ball, demonstrating a restored capacity to play games, to run, and to engage in competitive sports. Yet, one becomes aware of a second symbolism, more profound, that this sphere represents his small world of friends, family, home, hospital, and school. Immediately behind him in bas relief is the earth. It symbolizes the world and its people, to which the influence of Jesus Christ, his work, and his teaching has and will spread. It encompasses his love for humanity and especially his love for the children.

The group at the observer's right portrays the children of the Holy Land seeking help from the Savior. The kneeling girl leads her lame brother to be healed. The woman in the background holds a blind child with a bandage over the eyes. The baby in arms represents illness in infancy. Space limits the artist in his portrayal of the many afflicted and infirm people which Jesus treated and restored to health by miracles during his ministry in Palestine.

The group on the viewer's left portrays Christ during his ministry in the Western Hemisphere, with both Nephite and Lamanite children. "Jesus Christ did show himself unto the people of Nephi, as the multitude were gathered together in the land Bountiful, and did minister unto them." (3 Nephi preceding 11.) After teaching and admonishing the multitude, he offered to bless any who were sick or afflicted. All those who were brought to him were healed. They wept in gratitude, bowed down and kissed his feet. He then asked to have their little children brought to him.

The sculptor has modeled a re-enactment of this moment of Book of Mormon history in a moving and compassionate masterpiece. It is truly appropriate for a hospital, since those who strive to heal the children embrace the same spirit as the Savior made manifest.

Centerpiece of statuary, I Am Well Now

110

The Primary Children's Hospital panel

And it came to pass that he commanded that their little children should be brought. So they brought their little children and set them down upon the ground round about him, and Jesus stood in the midst; and the multitude gave way till they had all been brought unto him. And it came to pass that when they had all been brought, and Jesus stood in the midst, he commanded the multitude that they should kneel down upon the ground. And it came to pass that when they had knelt upon the ground, Jesus groaned within himself, and said: Father, I am troubled because of the wickedness of the people of the house of Israel. And when he had said these words, he himself knelt upon the earth; and behold he prayed unto the Father, and the things which he prayed cannot be written, and the multitude did bear record who heard him. And after this manner do they bear record: The eye hath never seen, neither hath the ear heard, before, so great and marvelous things as we saw and heard Jesus speak unto the Father; And no tongue can speak, neither can there be written by any man, neither can the hearts of men conceive so great and marvelous things as we both saw and heard Jesus speak; and no one can conceive of the joy which filled our souls at the time we heard him pray for us unto the Father. (3 Nephi 17:17.)

111

Christ blessing Nephite and Lamanite Children

Children in the Holy Land seeking help from The Savior

112

A MONUMENT TO PEACE

Peace I leave with you, my peace I give unto you: not as the world giveth, give I unto you. Let not your heart be troubled, neither let it be afraid.

John 14:27

And lift up an ensign of peace, and make a proclamation of peace unto the ends of the earth.

Doctrine and Covenants 105:39

Although there are over seventy references to Peace in the Holy Bible, it is unfortunate that Christ's admonitions for peace have not consistently been heeded. Peace should be and can be a positive force, but it must be promoted with national motivations and energies. There must be a conviction that conflict is not inevitable.

This monument was dedicated on Veterans Day 1976, the bicentennial year of the Declaration of Independence. The description by the sculptor, is appropriate to contemplate.

While we think of the ideals and the necessities which prompted our forefathers to proclaim LIBERTY and struggle to make such a reality two hundred years ago - It is timely now that we as a people advance ideals of similar worth and far reaching significance for our times and for the inspiration and guidance of future generations.

We are now in an era of peace and our contacts with other nations are those of hoping to maintain such; also to promote and advance understandings and better relationships among the nations of the world.

Therefore, it is appropriate that in the International Peace Gardens we erect a memorial to - PEACE - not only peace to ourselves but to extend this ideal unto all nations: as an international symbol and an international concept, put forth and produced in enduring materials and of artistic values which manifest masterful qualities; enduring and of great import.

As one will enter the Peace Gardens ... there will be seen... to the North, the beautiful Peace Memorial, heroic in size and heroic in concept. ... The pedestal and shaft are made ... (in cast stone) of rose quartz (aggregate), a material as hard as granite and as beautiful as the evening sky. In the morning, the crystals will stand out like jewels.

At the base of the pedestal, in front, is the symbol of the Sun breaking through the clouds. Shooting upwards are rays of bronze. Above the clouds is the inscription: The Dawn of a New Era which we must keep uppermost in our minds: and which we must strive to bring forth.

Above this is a beautifully sculptured figure ... to represent PEACE. In her right hand she holds the World, beneath which are bronze letters stating PEACE ON EARTH. In her left hand she holds a flaming torch; a symbol of our quests through knowledge, enlightenment and our activities. In her hair is an olive wreath, a crown also to symbolize PEACE. The countenance of the lady is lovely and serene; all of which we come to know and sense when we live in peace.

On the west (face) of the great shaft is an impressive group of children; a boy standing holds a kite, kites which fly high in the air gives us a feeling of soaring to great heights. So may our youths be free in mind and dare to have high aspirations beyond where they stand. In the boy's left hand is a wheel, meaning progress on earth. The boy looks to the figure above with the assurance of futures.

In front of the boy is a young girl caring for a little brother, characteristic of the feminine tender feelings and of homelike attention. The young child looks up into her eyes with trust and confidence. Above this group, full of thought and meanings is an inscription:

Our Hope for the Children

And indeed, our hope for the children is that we will leave to them as a lasting heritage to, "the DAWN OF A NEW ERA", our great contribution to civilization.

Avard T. Fairbanks

There are many monuments to War, but very few have been unveiled for Peace. This project was sponsored by the Salt Lake Council of Women. It was a very low budget endeavor, and appreciation was given to some who contributed talents and material. The foundation was placed there by the Breitling Brothers and the Jacobsen Construction companies. The pedestal and shaft were made and erected by the Buehner Company. Avard F. Fairbanks the sculptors son and Peter Fillerup, an aspiring young sculptor, served as an assistants.

A Monument to Peace

114

Monument to Peace, details of Our Hope for the Children

115

ARCHICONFRATERNITA DELLA MISERICORDIA

While residing and studying Art in Florence Italy, Avard Fairbanks and his family were occasionally awakened in the early morning hours by the chanting of a solemn procession of men dressed in robes with hoods sometimes in black and other times in white. They always appeared to be following a funeral bier on the way to a cemetery through narrow streets dimly lit by the torches which some carried.

The artist curiously inquired of acquaintances as to the significance of these marches. Were these for a person of importance recently deceased? He was answered that these processions were by men of the Misericordia, (fraternity of mercy). When they wore white robes, the funeral marches were for members of their order- the Archiconfraternita Della Misericordia. When they wore black robes, it was for paupers or the unclaimed dead, giving tribute in death to those who had nothing in life.

The solemn beauty of the pageantry impressed the sculptor sufficiently that he sought more information and was promptly directed to the headquarters of this Fraternity of Mercy, where he was cordially received. Several of the leading members proudly explained their history, their purpose, and their accomplishment.

This Florentine organization was founded about 1240 AD by Andrea Gallerani and is one of the World's oldest Christian lay orders. It's members, who feel honored to belong, are drawn from all walks of life. They volunteer their services for the care of the poor and the ill. Prior to going on duty, members pray in an oratory. They wear black robes and cowls when assisting the injured and infirm to emphasize their anonymity. The order owns ambulances and hearses, and the members rotate turns for volunteer assistance so that one rarely serves twice with the same college in the same unit. In a busy year, the order may respond to 75,000 calls for aid.

Besides their modern Samaritan-like assistance to the public, the order's record of services notes nursing care rendered to the victims and burial of the dead during medieval plagues and epidemics. During the Cholera epidemic of 1855 the Fraternity of Mercy attended 50,000 victims. In 1944 they provided the only ambulance service during the bombardment of the city in World War II.

Their deeds recall the admonitions of Paul to Timothy and to the Colossians:

> Now the end of the commandment is charity out of a pure heart, and of a good conscience, and of faith unfeigned.

> I Timothy 1:5.

> And above all these things put on charity, which is the bond of perfectness.

> And let the peace of God rule in your hearts, to the which also ye are called in one body; and be ye thankful.

> Let the word of Christ dwell in you richly in all wisdom; teaching and admonishing one another in psalms and hymns and spiritual songs, singing with grace in your hearts to the Lord.

> Colossians 3:14-16.

Besides profound community respect, these hooded benefactors are granted ancient privileges as their only reward. The city gates may be opened at night at their request, and they may attend those condemned to death, or assist released criminals.

After listening to their history and traditions, the sculptor told them he was planning to model a study in sculpture, portraying their procession. They seemed delighted at the suggestion and several of the officers volunteered to pose in their robes. The statuette, one fourth life size, was modeled in plastiline, cast in plaster, and then into bronze. It portrays three men leading a procession of mercy. The two torch bearers walk beside the central figure carrying a banner, each one chanting solemn prayers of supplication.

Archiconfraternita Della Misericordia

117

A MONUMENT TO DOMINGUEZ AND ESCALANTE

The expedition of Padre Antanasio Dominguez and Padre Silvestre Velez de Escalante guided by an indian boy named Joaquin was organized in the mission at Santa Fe. They led the first Christian missionary expedition into the Great Basin, seeking an overland route to the mission in Monterey, California. Padre Dominguez, a Franciscan monk, was the leader and Padre Escalante maintained a detailed diary of the journey. Their aim was to christianize the native people while establishing communications through the southern Rocky Mountains.

The expedition left Santa Fe July 29, 1776 with nine members and a flock of sheep for food. The long arduous trek traversed some of the some of the most barren, difficult and forbidding terrain on the continent. They had traveled north through what is the southwest corner of Colorado, then West to the valleys of Utah. The small group arrived at what is now the city of Spanish Fork in the Utah Valley, September 23, 1776.

With Winter approaching and mountain ranges to the West, they chose to turn South rather than to risk a journey through the mountains. Fearing attacks through the night, Joaquin would cry out, in his native tongue, "We are not Comanches." The trail went South to about the Utah Arizona border and turned East. The Grand Canyon was a barrier, but they found a crossing and proceed to the northeast Arizona. They returned to Santa Fe on January 3, 1777.

The monument, erected in 1976 commemorates the 200th anniversary of the entry into Utah Valley by the first White people in recorded history. It symbolizes the foresight and determination to expand horizons and to make Christian philosophy available to native people. It stands as a reminder of our heritage as a free people, that regardless of race or creed, people with a purpose have worked together to establish this great nation under God.

Monument Commemorating the 200th Anniversary
of the Dominguez-Escalante Expedition of 1776

119

SAINT GREGORY

One of the most influential leaders in early Christian history was Pope Gregory I, also referred to as Gregory the Great. The Scion (heir) of a very affluent family, he chose to dedicate his life to the Church. Appointed to be Pope at the age of 26, (the youngest ever), Gregory continued to serve in that capacity for sixty four years. He stressed the idea of penance as essential to the remission of sins and taught that purgatory was a place where even the righteous must suffer for minor offenses on order to be purified for admission into heaven. The Gregorian chant is ascribed by tradition to Pope Gregory.

This sculpture in cast stone is an integral part of the entrance of St. Gregory's Chapel in Phoenix Arizona. It was modeled in a formal style to conform to the architecture. When officials first saw the plans, they indicated disappointment at such a young face, but when the fact of Gregory's youthful ordination was presented, there was an enthusiastic acceptance. The Chapel is at a Boy's School, and serves as an appropriate inspiration.

The sculpture was created by Justin Fairbanks and his father, Avard.

Saint Gregory, the Great

120

LETTERS FROM PIETRASANTA

Chiesa Vecchio, (Ancient Church)

One Sunday afternoon here in Pietrasanta, Italy, I took a walk into the countryside and came upon a cemetery (cimitero) by the side of the road. The gates were open so I took the opportunity to go in and there view the grave sites. Many persons were there in remembrance of the loved ones passed on.

Greys Elegy could awaken thoughts of people here, and of what might be written if feelings of a master of literature could voice sentiments of this campasanta. There were numerous angels in marble to be seen here and there, which attracted my attention. Fresh flowers had been recently placed by those who remember their dead and for those whose partings from this life were more recent.

One exit faced a road leading to one of the hill towns. I took an extended walk for in the distance a church tower attracted my attention. It intrigued me. It looked old and I felt it might have history. Coming closer one could see that it was very old, to be sure. Then as I came closer to it there was a sign saying it was begun in 776 A.D. Similar dates passed through my mind.

776 B.C. was the date of the first Olympiad of Greece, the date of calculation of Greek history. 772 B.C. was the founding of Rome, the date of Roman calculation of their history.

Almost the same distance of time or near the meridian of our calculation of years before and after Christ. How strange I thought, now wasn't this date 776 A.D. in the time of what we call the Dark Ages. Christians had moved far from Rome. Here where I stood, they were away from the conquered Romans in an area not mentioned in general histories but where people lived and built a church to worship their God; their belief in Christianity. Villages in the hilltops and by the sea not far away can explain many possible events. Even recent times when fugitives took to the mountains during the 2nd World War, give explanations what could have occurred. This area was in conflict during the German occupation and the Italian rebellion against the Germans. Why and what might have occurred in the Dark Ages of long ago?

There are ruins of castles not far away, but this small church, though old, is not in ruins. The sign said restorations have been made at various times. So there were happenings here even in what we call the Dark Ages - and maybe even before then. If so who were the people? What were they doing?

Not far away are great mountains, high and grand. Not far to the north is Carrara, Colona Forte d Marni, and Pietrasanta.

A CHRISTMAS LETTER TO THE FAMILY

Pietrasanta, Italy
Cara Mia: (My Dear Ones)
15 Dicembre, 1974

This evening I am watching the sunset glow. From my window it is flooding the hills behind this little city famous for its great works of marble and to which the great sculptors of the world came to have their choice works of art made in the finest of all materials.

The villinos and villas dot the hillsides and near to the top are two little towns, Capriglia and Capezzano.

The light tinted houses reflect the golden sunset. They stand out among the cypress, olive, pines and other trees. The windows here and there of the houses reflect the sunshine. This glow will last but a short time.

On one nearby hill is the old villa of the Medici. It is not entirely in ruins, but much of its splendor is gone.

To the left and behind this antique place, the tall mountains of marble reach upward. There are mountains where Michaelangelo found the choice marble and started the quarries which have continued to furnish to the world the finest of marble for buildings and for works of art.

Now the evening is becoming darker and the night is coming on. The hills show a faint silhouette against a deep dark blue sky. Where the houses could be seen there are lights which appear like giant stars in constellations in the heavens.

The bells of the Campanile of the Duomo of Pietrasanta are now ringing. (They toll the nell of parting day) and also ring out the near approach of

Natale Christmas which is only ten days away.

I cannot help but think of home and the joys of the Christmas times our family has had together. We are now separated. Our children have their families and now live in various cities in our country. However, we all think of one another and realize how happiness is expanded to our loved ones to their children and now to their little ones. What joys will there be across the seas and oceans.

Though I am far away, I am thinking of home. I hope this letter reaches you before Christmas and brings to all my greetings.

With love to all, Father, Grandfather,
and Great Grandfather.

ALONE AT CHRISTMAS IN ITALY

Just now, I am looking out from the window of the casa, (house) where I am staying here in Pietrasanta, Italy this Christmas Day 1975. Quite a distance beyond this immediate foreground of red tile roof tops there is a mist over the green of the trees in the countryside which reaches out a few miles to the shore of the Mediterranean Sea. The mist which settles down is the atmosphere which comes in from this great body of water. It is a very delicate light color of blue. Through it can be seen variations of tree tops. They are interspersed with houses here and there, which gives sort of a mottled texture of iridescence. Then at the coast there is a broad shining streak of water, the Tyrrhenian Sea, (this is part of the Mediterranean Sea). The scene is beautiful and thrilling; especially as one sees the red tile roofs below the middle ground of blue and the brilliant yellow sky above - the primary colors in grandeur and in harmony.

The time is 3:30 in the afternoon. The sun gives forth a brilliant glow; just before the golden evening comes on. Here and there the chimneys emit their white and grey smoke from rooms below. Such is evidence of Christmas cheer and family festivities in the houses, and that home life here is joyful.

Houses are in rows all built up against each other along narrow streets. They are quite different to the separate houses we have in our residential areas in the United States. They all seem like city buildings of 3 or 4 stories.

Imagination arises of the many happy people, some sitting at firesides, children enjoying gifts and still others relaxing. The usual roar and bustle of the streets below are more silent today. A calmness is felt throughout.

I am alone in my room away from folks at home, so I am in a contemplative mood. This Christmas is unusual, to be sure! The friends, here where I stay, have gone away for the day so all is calm and quiet. I have therefore this opportunity to ponder upon many past Christmas times.

Some years ago here in Italy, I created a study of the Madonna and in her arms a child; Christ our Lord. This I carved in rose marble. At another time I carved again in Portuguese rose marble the same study. It was beautiful and a very choice work of art. So today, I am designing a setting for this marble Madonna.

While in Italy, one cannot help but be impressed with the love of the people here for Mary, the mother of the Savior. This subject has had predominant influences in the development of the great Renaissance in History which brought about a golden age of civilization. I am deeply impressed - as particularly at this moment I look out of the window to the western sky. It is becoming golden. The shimmering of the sea is a beautiful strata of unusual splendor, reflecting back the sun's great glow.

As I look westward, I ponder upon the deep significance of Christmas and the birth of the Savior, of all mankind, and the promise for eternal life! Will we today have a Golden Age of our century? Will our culture reflect, as does the sea, the glory of the heavens and celestial existence?

Piercing through the blue mist and into the golden sky above is a beautiful campanile. I now am looking at it. Its bells ring out. The red tile of the rooftops are now turning purple intone, because they are in shadow. The bell tower was erected in the times of the Renaissance.

This tower is not just made of stone and mortar. It has an upward reach and meaning. It was built within a monastery, however today it is within the grounds of a church school for young people. Rays of the evening sky are now shining through the belfry. As seen from the shadow side, it is becoming more firm and sturdy in appearance.

I have taken the opportunity at this time of the day to go upon to the rooftop where there is a platform. Before me now is a panorama, westward towards the sea. Then I gaze north, south, and east. Here I look toward the high hills and the mountains beyond. The immediate hills are covered with olive, chestnut, and pine trees, and other varieties. Nearby are houses built up against each other with open spaces where narrow streets meander. Here and there between the trees as one sees beyond this small city, are farm houses and small gardens where some of the marble carvers live, also the cantadini (small farmers).

On top of the hill closest to Pietrasanta is to be seen the old summer villa of the Medici family. It was within the city walls. It dominated the surrounding area. It was not a castle but more like a palace. Remains of it are still usable and livable but its former splendor is gone, a part of the old city wall goes up to the hillside to this villa. Some of the houses in this city have been built up against the old walls. The Medici Family was the patron of Michaelangelo. It was from here that he searched in the mountains for the best marble. Quarries which he started are still in operation for obtaining the finest of statuary marble.

Beyond the Medici villa and on higher hills are two little villages, Capriglia and Capezzano. The windows from houses way up high are reflecting the golden sunshine; as if telegraphing back messages to heaven of peace in the houses (here on Earth as in Heaven) on this day Natale celebrating the birth of our Savior. Soon the many signaling windows will be dark again as the sun is setting. Later, lights will shine out from them, more signals of happy homes on the hills.

Behind the hills are the great and rugged mountains of marble, (which can serve the World for hundreds or thousands of years). The sun still shines on them because of their height. They capture the last rays. The white, now rose in color, on these high peaks is like snow on our western mountains. However, the white is marble and has all the appearance of perpetual snow. Now the mountains are taking on a deep blue color against the sky. The stars are beginning to twinkle.

The marble of these great mountains has long been called sacred or santa. Stone is called pietra, hence this city was named Pietrasanta or stone sacred.

The bells of Pietrasanta now ring out, the day is over. The sun has gone down beyond the sea. It is out over the ocean. At home the sun is rising over our mountains, Christmas morning.

So Christmas Greetings to dear ones.

Avard Fairbanks

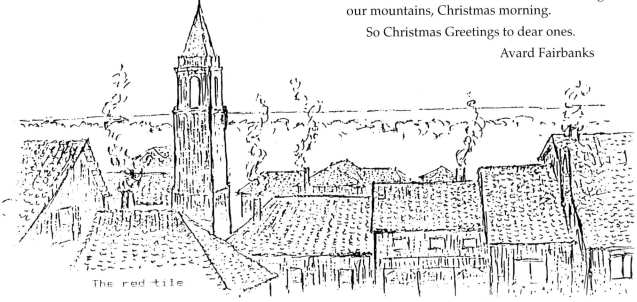

The red tile

ART AND RELIGIOUS PHILOSOPHY

In his Fine Art teaching career, Avard T. Fairbanks repeatedly stressed to his students the concern for quality. This applied not only to craftmanship but also to design and content. Art to Dr. Fairbanks was a means of expression, a communication from the artist to the observer. He taught that a fine artist must be both a skilled craftsman and a creative intellectual, well trained in science, philosophy and literature. In the realm of religious artistic expression, he felt the artist must have a profound comprehension of spiritual motivation. Those who fail to grasp divine principles are easily overwhelmed by religious perspective. Addressing this issue, Dr. Fairbanks wrote:

Some people with primitive thinking view in religion the phenomena of this world with an awesome perspective. Their fears become guides to their conduct. Primitive religions work upon peoples primitive fears. That is why the behaviors and ethics of these people have been geared up to "hell, fire, brimstone, and damnation," threats essentially to pain and punishments. Other People, when gaining knowledge of natural laws begin to believe that religion is out of date, have no more use for it, and turn to mechanistic philosophies. Yet another group of people can see religion in it's greater aspect, in essentially the same manner as they may comprehend science.

With Man advancing beyond the primitive, there are those who believe they are above the factors which gave them hope in a world of struggle. Bearing an attitude of belonging to the "upper crust", they rationalize frequently against religion. These with a pedantic sophistication have gained a complex of superiority, and they have a desire to exhibit or "show off", this attitude of superiority. Sometimes they manifest this by braggadocio if they be bullies; by pseudo-science if they be intelligencia; or by aestheticism if they be dilettantes.

Some persons, through study use reason. Then they accord religion to their metaphysical studies or to scientific understanding. There are also those, who through their studies, discredit religion altogether when their concepts of religion are not beyond the primitive level.

There are others who expect in religion the completely unnatural events and effects. They are the miracle seekers always wanting a great phenomena or spectacular occurence to fulfill their needs.

Now those who have Faith have found the True Path, and the sure one, Science may help, and Philosophies may assist by reason. Miracles may occur to strengthen faith. But Faith and the Love of God, as our Father in Heaven, transcends all else.

In all nature, man only is a skilled creator. He has creative powers not found in any of the other living animals. He can handle material substance through his understanding of natural laws, and he can utilize these laws. By the combining of matter into ratios and proportions, which he has learned by Study and through experimental efforts, he can bring formations into being. Thus, Man is a creator.

Therefore, man in mind is a product of God who claims him, for God created man in his own image. Did God create man only in physical form? Too many people can only see this kind of interpretation of the words in the bible. In mind God also gave man the qualities of himself. So Man became a living soul.

Now realize the true meaning of a soul. It is not just physical being nor spirit apart from the body. The soul is spirit and substance, and man walks by faith, he moves by faith, and by faith he comes to know his eternal Father in heaven.

Not by fear, not by magic or miracles, and not by rationalization, nor by earthly science, but man, by understanding through his own efforts exercises Faith in things known - those truths revealed - as well as the unknown. The profound thinker in the realms of the true religion believing that, "The Glory of God is Intelligence," has faith in his own being, created as a Son of God with potentials of his Father in Heaven.

Avard T. Fairbanks

SACRED SCULPTURE BY STUDENTS

This bas relief sculpture composition was created by Mrs. Elaine Brockbank Evans from Holladay, Utah, a student of Avard Fairbanks at the University of Michigan. Mrs. Evans has taught art and has created many other fine studies in sculpture.

DAVID AND SAUL

But the Spirit of the Lord departed from Saul, and an evil spirit from the Lord troubled him.

And Saul's servants said unto him, Behold now, an evil spirit from God troubleth thee.

Let our lord now command thy servants, which are before thee, to seek out a man, who is a cunning player on an harp: and it shall come to pass, when the evil spirit from God is upon thee, that he shall play with his hand, and thou shalt be well.

And David came to Saul, and stood before him: and he loved him greatly; and he became his armor bearer...

And it came to pass, when the evil spirit of God was upon Saul, that David took an harp, and played with his hand: so Saul was refreshed, and was well, and the evil spirit departed from him.

I Samuel 16:14-23

This composition in sculpture was created by Dorothy I. Munro, of Fairfield, Iowa, a student of Avard Fairbanks at the University of Michigan.

RUTH

During a famine in Bethlehem, Elimelech and his wife, Naomi, and their two sons left their home and went to the land of Moab. There Elimelech died and left Naomi with the two sons, Mahlon and Chilion. In due time, both these sons took wives who were of Moab. Their names were Orpah and Ruth. When the sons also died, Naomi chose to return to Bethlehem from Moab. She advised her daughters in law to return home to their mothers, after which she kissed them and wept. Orpah chose first to follow Naomi, but was dissuaded and returned to her home. Ruth declined twice and said, "Intreat me not to leave thee, or to return from following after thee: for whither thou goest I will go; and where thou lodgest, I will lodge: thy people shall be my people, and thy God My God: (Ruth 1:16) So they went on their way until they came to Bethlehem.

They arrived at the beginning of barley harvest. Ruth offered to go gleaning in the fields. It was the custom to allow the poor to glean the fields after the reapers had harvested the crop. She was kindly received by Boaz, a kinsman of Elimelech, for her loyalty to Noami. The story of Ruth exemplifies the strength of family bonds, and is symbolized by the harvest of wheat and barley.

ONE WORLD

One World, a statue of Christ holding the World in his hands, was designed to symbolize the Spirit of Christ as a means of promoting world unity. This compassionate study portraying Christ with affection and concern for people of all the world was created by Mrs. Agnes McLean of Ann Arbor, Michigan, a student of Avard Fairbanks at the University of Michigan. This heroic statue in bronze was placed on the grounds of the Methodist Home for Old People in Chelsea, Michigan in 1946. It was mounted on a pedestal of rainbow granite. The rainbow colors symbolizes the Biblical promise of hope and a brighter future. In front of the statue, a 20 foot pool was constructed. A continuous flow of water springing up from a well was designed to symbolize everlasting life, reminiscent of the parable the Savior taught the Samaritan woman at Jacob's Well (John 4:4-42).

SKETCHES

HAGOTH, THE BUILDER OF SHIPS

Before Avard T. Fairbanks created a monument on any subject, he would submit careful sketches, drawings in pencil, and often pen and ink to prospective sponsors. He was also often requested to make illustrations of events recorded in biblical or Book of Mormon scriptures. This pen and ink drawing appeared on the cover of The Improvement Era, September 1950, published by the Church of Jesus Christ of Latter-Day Saints. It portrayed Hagoth, the Builder of Ships.

Alma, chapter 63 of the Book of Mormon , tells of Hagoth building ships for carrying people north from the land of Zarahemla. Some ships did not return, and were assumed lost at sea. Considering the prevailing Equatorial Currents, these ships could have drifted West and made landfall on islands of the Pacific. It is thought that these Nephites who departed from the west coast of South or Central America intending to migrate to northern territory, may be ancestors of the Polynesians. This inadvertent dispersal would fulfill the prophesy of Lehi, who blessed his young son, Joseph and promised that his seed shall not be destroyed.

SHEPHERDS ABIDING IN THE FIELD

And she brought forth her first born son, and wrapped him in swaddling clothes, and laid him in a manger; because there was no room for them in the inn.

And there were in the same country shepherds abiding in the field, keeping watch over their flock by night.

And, lo, the angel of the Lord came upon them, and the glory of the Lord shone round about them: and they were sore afraid.

And the angel said unto them, Fear not: for, behold, I bring you good tidings of great joy, which shall be to all people.

For unto you is born this day in the city of David a Saviour, which is Christ the Lord.

And it came to pass, as the angels were gone away from them into heaven, the shepherds said one to another, Let us now go even unto Bethlehem, and see this thing which is come to pass, which the Lord hath made known unto us.
Luke 2: 7-11, 15

This drawing was created by Jonathan L. Fairbanks, a son of Avard Fairbanks and was used as a Christmas greeting card. It portrays the annunciation of the birth of Jesus Christ to the shepherds.

WIST YE NOT THAT I MUST BE ABOUT MY FATHER'S BUSINESS?

As a youth, Jesus accompanied his parents to Jerusalem for the Feast of the Passover. When Joseph and Mary began their trip homeward, and found their son was not with them, they assumed him to be among their kinfolk and traveled on. By the next day they realized he was missing from the group, and they turned back to Jerusalem to find him.

> And it came to pass, that after three days they found him in the temple, sitting in the midst of the doctors, both hearing them, and asking them questions.

> And all that heard him were astonished at his understanding and answers.

> And when they saw him they were amazed: and his mother said unto him, Son, why hast thou thus dealt with us? behold, thy father and I have sought thee sorrowing.

> And he said unto them, How is it that ye sought me? wist ye not that I must be about my Father's business?

> Luke 2:46-49

In the folio of sketches was found this plan for another statue. Avard Fairbanks was planning more sculpture than time allowed him to complete. This moment of Christ's life caused concern for his parents, but became a joyful reunion.

SWORDS TO PLOUGHSHARES

And it shall come to pass in the last days, that the mountain of the Lord's house shall be established in the top of the mountains, and shall be exalted above the hills; and all nations shall flow unto it.

And many people shall go and say, Come ye, and let us go up to the mountain of the Lord, to the house of the God of Jacob; and he will teach us of his ways, and we will walk in his paths: for out of Zion shall go forth the law, and the word of the Lord from Jerusalem.

And he shall judge among the nations, and shall rebuke many people: and they shall beat their swords into plowshares, and their spears into pruninghooks: nation shall not lift up sword against nation, neither shall they learn war any more.

Isaiah 2:2-4

This sketch from the sculptor's drawing board portrays the prophesy of Isaiah for the last days, when many of the primitive impulses of men will have been overcome by teachings of righteousness, a belief in a better way of life, and a promised heavenly reward. Avard Fairbanks sketched this as a proposal for a monument in the Holy Land.

John the Revelator

"And I saw another angel fly in the midst of heaven, having the everlasting gospel to preach unto them
that dwell on the earth, and to every nation, and kindred, and tongue, and people." Revelations 14: 6

129

MADONNA AND CHILD

And suddenly there was with the angel a multitude of the heavenly host praising God and saying,

Glory to God in the highest, and on Earth peace, good will toward men.

Luke 2: 13-14

The Madonna and Child have been a favorite subject for many artists, both painters and sculptors. Here as the mother gazes admiringly at the beautiful infant, and he looks up securely in her protective embrace, the strong bond of love between the mother and child is gracefully portrayed.

This life size sculpture was modeled in bas relief with it's companion piece, Christ among the Doctors, for Fred Zeder of Grosse Pointe, Michigan, former Chief Engineer and later Chairman of the Board of the Chrysler Corporation. He in turn presented them to his church.

It was modeled in clay and cast first as a positive then as intaglio in the same manner as the companion piece, Christ Among the Doctors. Several copies were made of each one. This negative or intaglio has the features reversed and recessed. Illumination from below accentuates the same lines and creates the same shadows as those of a cameo or positive when the light is from above. The effect is surprising, with the illusion of even greater depth than the more common cameo bas relief.

Madonna and Child

CHRIST AMONG THE DOCTORS

And when he was twelve years old, they went up to Jerusalem after the custom of the feast.

And when they had fulfilled the days, as they returned, the child Jesus tarried behind in Jerusalem; and Joseph and his mother knew not of it.

But they, supposing him to have been in the company, went a days journey; and they sought him among their kinfolk and acquaintance.

And when they found him not, they turned back again to Jerusalem, seeking him.

And it came to pass, that after three days they found him in the temple, sitting in the midst of the doctors, both hearing them, and asking them questions.

And all that heard him were astonished at his understanding and answers.

And when they saw him, they were amazed: and his mother said unto him, Son, why hast thou thus dealt with us? behold, thy father and I have sought thee sorrowing.

And he said unto them, How is it that ye sought me? wist ye not that I must be about my Father's business?

And they understood not the saying which he spake unto them....but his mother kept these sayings in her heart.

And Jesus increased in wisdom and stature, and in favour with God and man.

Luke 2: 42-52

This sacred sculpture was modeled in bas relief and cast in the usual manner, with a plaster mold which was a negative. A border was then modeled around this mold, and a gelatin mold, (commonly termed glue mold) which is flexible, was poured on the negative relief. Using this flexible glue mold, which had a positive image, several intaglio casts were made. These casts then had a negative or recessed image of an intalgio relief.

When it is illuminated from below the shadows fall in the same places as those of the more common cameo relief illuminated from above. At a distance it gives an appearance as though it were cameo bas relief. On closer inspection, the observer is pleasantly surprised at the illusion.

This is a companion piece to the Madonna and child. Both were modeled, cast in the same manner, and finished with an oak frame for Mr. Fred Zeder, formerly Chief Engineer and later Chairman of the Board of the Chrysler Corporation. Both sculptured reliefs, in time, were later placed on display at Mr. Zeder's Church.

Christ Among the Doctors

"I Am the Resurrection and the Life"

When Lazarus of Bethany was gravely ill, his sisters, Martha and Mary, sent for Jesus, hoping that he would save their brother's life. When Jesus heard that his friend was sick, he remained two days longer in the place where he was. He asked his disciples to follow him to Judea. They were reluctant, as the Jews had recently sought to stone him. He reassured his disciples and announced that Lazarus was already dead.

When Jesus came to Bethany, Lazarus had already been entombed four days. Martha went to meet Jesus when she heard he was coming.

> Then said Martha unto Jesus, Lord, if thou hadst been here, my brother had not died. But I know, that even now, whatsoever thou wilt ask of God, God will give it thee. Jesus saith unto her, Thy brother shall rise again. Martha saith unto him, I know that he shall rise again in the resurrection at the last day. Jesus said unto her, I am the resurrection, and the life: he that believeth in me, though he were dead, yet shall he live: And whosoever liveth and believeth in me shall never die. Believest thou this? She saith unto him, Yea, Lord: I believe that thou art the Christ, the Son of God, which should come into the world.

(John 11:21-27.)

"I Am the Resurrection and the Life"

135

Martha returned and spoke to her sister Mary, telling her Jesus had come. Mary also came to Jesus, fell down weeping at his feet, and said:

Lord, if thou hadst been here, my brother had not died. When Jesus therefore saw her weeping, . . . he groaned in the spirit, and was troubled, And said, Where have ye laid him? They said unto him, Lord, come and see. Jesus wept.... Jesus therefore again groaning in himself cometh to the grave. It was a cave, and a stone lay upon it. Jesus said, Take ye away the stone. Martha saith unto him, Lord, by this time he stinketh: for he hath been dead four days. Jesus saith unto her, Said I not unto thee, that, if thou wouldest believe thou shouldest see the glory of God ? Then they took away the stone from the place where the dead was laid. And Jesus lifted up his eyes, and said, Father, I thank thee that thou hast heard me. And I knew that thou hearest me always: but because of the people which stand by I said it, that they may believeth that thou hast sent me. And when he thus had spoken, he cried with a loud voice, Lazarus, come forth. And he that was dead came forth, bound hand and foot with graveclothes.

(John 11:32-35; 38-44.)

"I Am the Resurrection and the Life" close up

137

THE HOLY SACRAMENT

Then came the day of unleavened bread, when the passover must be killed.

And he sent Peter and John, saying, Go and prepare us the passover, that we may eat.

And they said unto him, Where wilt thou that we prepare?

And he said unto them, Behold, when ye are entered into the city, there shall a man meet you, bearing a pitcher of water; follow him unto the house where entereth in.

And ye shall say unto the goodman of the house, The Master saith unto thee, Where is the guestchamber, where I shall eat the passover with my disciples?

And he shall shew you a large upper room furnished: there make ready.

And they went, and found as he had said unto them: and they made ready the passover.

And when the hour was come, he sat down, and the twelve apostles with him.

And he said unto them, With desire I have desired to eat this passover with you before I suffer:

For I say unto you, I will not any more eat thereof, until it be fulfilled in the kingdom of God.

And he took the cup, and gave thanks, and said, Take this, and divide it among yourselves:

For I say unto you, I will not drink of the fruit of the vine, until the kingdom of God shall come.

And he took bread, and gave thanks, and brake it, and gave unto them, saying This is my body which is given for you: this do in remembrance of me.

Likewise also the cup after supper, saying, This cup is the new testament in my blood, which is shed for you.

Luke 22: 7-20

In this bas relief titled THE HOLY SACRAMENT the artist has modeled a figure representing Jesus Christ with the cup of wine that is to be passed to the disciples for each to drink, symbolizing his blood and life. A piece of unleavened bread is being offered, symbolic of his flesh, for the disciples to partake.

The Latin inscription below the feet is translated, "With the hand of our Lord," while the inscription on the halo means, "Here Is My Body." The two flanking figures on the right and left symbolize hope and sorrow respectively. Behind the central figure of Christ is the cross, the symbol of his death, which he had foretold. Behind it are Gothic arches, symbolic of the development of churches for worship. The two circles in the upper corners have twelve interior arcs representing the twelve disciples. In one circle is the temple of Jerusalem. The other circle represents a king holding a Bible and an offering of wine in a cup, indicating acceptance of the principles of Christ's teachings. Radiating beams from the halo number twelve on each side, which may also resemble the points of a compass signifying guidance.

There are two angels framing the central arch, one announcing with a clarion the precepts of the Lord and the other, with a sword and shield, defending it from the enemies of the faith. Capitols of the column supporting the arches on the right of the central figure have chalices with grape vines, for wine, while those on the left have wheat or barley, for bread. In one lesser arch is a lamb, symbolic of gentleness, while in the other is an eagle symbolic of courage, swiftness, and strength. The Eagle often symbolizes John the Evangelist, as the Lamb symbolizes the Savior.

The stand to the right has two Greek letters one resembling X, which is Chi and one resembling P which is Rho; together they are an abbreviation for Kyrios meaning Christ. When translated from Aramaic it means Prophesied King. The left has a compound symbol of a clover leaf, and a triangle, symbolic of the trinity, and of a dove representing the Holy Ghost.

Regardless of faith, the observer cannot but sense the solemn impact of the Holy Sacrament, and its message, in remembrance of the suffering of our Savior.

The Holy Sacrament

139

CHRIST IN COMPASSION

Jesus Christ expressed his concern and extended his love to mankind throughout his ministry. This portrait expresses his compassion for the people.

Come unto me, all ye that labour and are heavy laden, and I will give you rest.

Take my yoke upon you, and learn of me; for I am meek and lowly in heart: and ye shall find rest unto your souls.

For my yoke is easy and my burden is light.

Matthew 11:28-30

JESUS IN MEDITATION

After the last supper, Jesus went to the Mount of Olives, then into the Garden of Gethsemane, followed by his disciples. These moments of meditation and prayer were recorded in the gospels written by Matthew and Luke. The portrayal is of Christ in profound thought, very solemn, but with an inspiring countenance. His thoughts in contemplation of prayer, sacred and personal, but for the benefit of mankind, are portrayed in his beautiful, radiant countenance.

And he came out, and went, as he was wont, to the mount of Olives; and his disciples also followed him.

And when he was at the place, he said unto them, Pray that ye enter not into temptation.

And he was withdrawn from them about a stone's cast, and kneeled down, and prayed,

Saying, Father, if thou be willing, remove this cup from me: nevertheless not my will, but thine be done.

And there appeared an angel unto him from heaven, strengthening him.

Luke 22:39-46

141

JESUS CHRIST AND THE SERMON ON THE MOUNT

In the summer of 1951, Avard Fairbanks sailed for Europe in order to make arrangements for future marble carvings as the war had disrupted former business contacts. At about this time, Justin, his fourth son, had completed a mission and the two were to meet in Italy. Justin had just made a tour through Egypt and Israel. Since the sculptor had never been there, he felt that this was a good opportunity for him to go. His first impression of Jerusalem is best described in a letter he sent to the family.

"Tonight I am writing from the ancient and Holy City, Jerusalem. Leaving Egypt was a very impressive sight. From the plane, I looked down upon the vast territory and saw the green valley of the Nile, then the yellow desert sands on both sides. Crossing the desert to the east, we approached the Red Sea. It is deep and blue, not red. We passed over Suez and the great canal. It is a sight to behold.

"I thought of Moses and his leading a throng of oppressed people. The desert is formidable, and for him to have taken them was a courageous task almost beyond conception. The Red Sea on the north makes two forks, and between are great mountains which arise particularly near the crotch of the fork. This is the Sinai Peninsula, and it was on Mt. Sinai where Moses received the Ten Commandments.

"To see all of this, one could review the life and struggles of a people and understand even details clearly (for even small bushes could be seen when they occasionally appeared) . There, from above, one can realize that if man can see details closely with encompassing much, what can be the possibility of God who from above can see and know all, even minute and personal matters. One could almost trace a route which Moses might have taken to lead the children of Israel away from Egypt and the Pharaoh.

'From the eastern fork of the Red Sea, the Gulf of Aquaba, we followed it toward the north to the promised land. First the Dead Sea (and there are really tall mountains around it), the plains near Jerico and then we flew toward the mountains west of the Jordan. In among the mountains or rather on the mountains is the city of Jerusalem. We descended on a plain nearby. The country is dryer than Utah, unless we think of Zion Canyon and the St. George country. Zion's Canyon is well-named for it is very dry like this land of Zion.

"I went to a little hotel recommended by Justin, but found that I happened to get another one where Arabs go. However, it was very good and clean. The people are very nice.

"This evening I went through the Damascus gate into the walled city of Jerusalem. I walked down the path of Christ, the streets where he carried his cross. I saw the building of Pontius Pilate, the court where the crown of thorns was placed on Christ's head, and where he was whipped. Then, along the way, I passed the place where Mary was born. Further traveling by foot, I walked on out of Herod's gate. There, in full view, was the Garden of Gethsemane and higher on the hill was the Mount of the Ascension.

"Twilight had come on, the evening was cool, a young man and an Arab walked with mc to show me the way. We went to the Garden of Gethsemane (of course it is walled in, and a church is built over the rock of agony), but another garden was off to the side and there I meditated on the great feelings of our Lord who sensed his fate. I lingered, absorbing the atmosphere, the history of Christ, and his emotions. The new moon was above the Jerusalem walls, the evening star was on the same diagonal line; it was most outstanding and impressive.

"An Arab and his daughter were nearby getting water from a well. I went over. I could not speak to him in his language, but the accompanying Arab did. I drank of the water and thought of Christ when he asked in his great prayer to his Father if it were possible to let this bitter cup pass, but thy will be done, was Christ's submission. After this eventful experience, I continued to climb the Mount of Ascension. It is a tall hill, but we climbed it. It is rocky, too. Houses are built along the way, like Fiesole in Italy.

"From one of the houses a little baby was crying. I recalled our song in Italy, Jesu Bambino Non Piange Piu (Little Jesus Do Not Cry). It was a long climb to the summit, darkness came on, the new moon gave a little light.

"There is an Arab Mosque on the spot of the ascension, but still the Arabs give recognition to Christ as a prophet.

Jesus Christ and the Sermon on the Mount

"I looked over Jerusalem; lights shone out sparsely; they were not brilliant. The great walls were dark. I stood near where Christ arose into heaven. I recalled: 'Ye men of Galilee, why stand ye gazing upward? Know ye not that this same Jesus which you see ascend, will in like manner descend?' Being far removed in time in history, but close to the actual scene, I wonder if I would also have been as dubious as the men of Galilee if I had lived then.

"Coming down the mountain I saw the lights of Jerusalem fade away as the walls seemed to arise. There were no more lights, but huge, dark walls. Then later the moon also was hidden and the evening star. As I continued down into the valley, the walls arose darker and more massive. Finally I reached the path leading back to the City. The great city was on the west and the mountain of Ascension was east. While standing there in awe and with deep feelings, I wondered if I might see the ascension. Just then the whole mountain lit up in a white light. A faster pulsation of heartbeat came, and a cold feeling like a chill or a slight electric shock came over me. (Of course, it was only the lights of an occasional automobile on one of the hill roads, but the illumination could not have been better timed if it had been on a stage set for a great drama.) I saw the light of the ascension glow and have had a thrill I shall never forget. The drama many years ago and the stage of great proportions are real in my mind. I can rearrange them and bring the two together tonight.

"I looked again on the top of the darkened mountain. My eyes saw only the stars above, Gethsemane in the middle ground, and cypress and olive trees in the foreground. My spirit felt the meaning of history and of Christ's mission. Again, my soul was filled with rejoicing. I marvel in the message of Christ's life, in having walked where our Savior walked in life on earth and in a resurrected state of being.

"A dog barks, which disturbs the quietness of the evening, dark figures of people pass by, and the pitter-patter of the sandaled feet on the pathway give a sort of rhythmic cadence to the music of the setting; the wind blows through the trees and causes a rustling. I am overwhelmed.

"I have returned to my room and am recording my feelings. It is late and all is silent as I look over Jerusalem. While I am writing, a cock crows three times. It is strange.

"I have experienced a Gethsemane. Tomorrow I visit the hill called Golgatha and then the Garden of the Tomb. I shall see the settings of the life of Christ our Savior.

"This is the Holy City of Jerusalem."

"My deepest love I send to all of you at home."

Avard

The next day he visited the Mount of Olives where Jesus often went to meditate. Here Christ admonished the apostles and foretold the great events of the coming of the Lord. Here he wept for Jerusalem. Surprisingly, there was no memorialization to these great moments. This Mount brings to mind another mountain overlooking the Sea of Galilee, where Jesus spoke to the multitude and chose the apostles.

During the ministry of Jesus of Nazareth, the sermon given on the Mount stands out as his greatest teaching and serves as a basis of Christian doctrine; it has been given less attention by artists, for his crucifixion is the more dramatic event. This statue, conceived and composed by Dr. Fairbanks, engenders the atmosphere of the moment when Jesus spoke the Beatitudes to the disciples held spellbound in awe. As recorded in the words of St. Matthew:

Blessed are the poor in spirit: for theirs is the kingdom of heaven.
Blessed are they that mourn: for they shall be comforted.
Blessed are the meek: for they shall inherit the earth.
Blessed are they which do hunger and thirst after righteousness: for they shall be filled.
Blessed are the merciful: for they shall obtain mercy.
Blessed are the pure in heart: for they shall see God.
Blessed are the peacemakers: for they shall be called the children of God.
Blessed are they which are persecuted for righteousness' sake: for theirs is the kingdom of heaven.
Blessed are ye, when men shall revile you, and persecute you, and shall say all manner of evil against you falsely, for my sake.
Rejoice, and be exceeding glad: for great is your reward in heaven: for so persecuted they the prophets which were before you. (Matthew 5:3-12.)
And it came to pass, when Jesus had ended these sayings, the people were astonished at his doctrine: For he taught them as one having authority, and not as the scribes. (Matthew 7:28-29.)

Colossal portrait of Jesus Christ

145

THE MISSION OF AVARD T. FAIRBANKS

While many of Avard Fairbanks' classmates were filling traditional missions in foreign fields, the young artist was modeling sculpture in Laiae, Hawaii for the soon to be completed Hawaiian Temple. This was a project in which he had joined his older brother, J. Leo Fairbanks on a contract made with L.D.S. Church architects for the Hawaiian Temple sculpture. The commission included four friezes on the temple; the twelve oxen for the Baptismal Font; and two other sculptures, one representing the Priesthood, and the other of Motherhood. J. Leo was a learned scholar of the Bible and Book of Mormon. The two brothers were able to put into the sculpture considerable expressive symbolism as well as portrayal of great characters of religious history. Avard's first heroic statue, and one of his greatest, "Lehi blessing Joseph", commands reverence from those who view it.

World War I was raging in Europe at the time, and in 1917 the United States became actively involved. This interfered with any plans for a mission which Avard might have cherished, but the missionary spirit, a zeal to proclaim by portrayal in sculpture continued throughout his career. In 1923 he created the monument to the Three Witnesses to the Book of Mormon which was place on Temple Square. This was modeled in Eugene, Oregon while he was teaching at the University there. In that city, He and his wife Maude joined with a few other Latter Day Saints to start the Eugene Branch of the Church which met for several years in the Odd Fellows Hall. That small branch has since flourished, progressed and become two Stakes.

After a few years in Oregon, Avard had the opportunity to study again in Europe. The family, including the four boys, traveled to Florence, Italy. In addition to family religious services in the home, visits were made to some of the chapels and cathedrals so that the young boys could experience the ancient traditions and better appreciate the restored gospel.

When he was appointed a professor of Sculpture at the University of Michigan, the family moved to Ann Arbor. Soon a small group of Saints began to meet in the family home. Later a branch was organized and meeting were held in a rented chapel. Avard was chosen to be the Branch President, and served many years. Presently the Ann Arbor area is also a Stake. Throughout those years, strong ties often called the

family to Utah. During one of those summer trips, Avard was requested to present a lecture at a meeting of the Daughters of the Utah Pioneers to be held in Big Cottonwood Canyon.

For a pioneer subject he recalled a sad story which had been passed down in the family. His Grandfather's oldest son had died in infancy and had been buried on the prairie. Similar incidents, of course, could have been recorded in many other pioneer families. This was then chosen as a theme, a young couple burying their infant in a shallow grave. The sculpture demonstration lecture was very impressive, and received many favorable comments.

On the way back to Michigan, a special effort was made to visit the site of Winter Quarters. The Cemetery was in disrepair and overgrown with weeds and tall grass. Appalled by this neglect, Avard resolved to do something to honor this hallowed ground.

The year was 1932, and preparations were being made in Chicago for a magnificent World Fair. When the Northern States Mission President, George Romney conducted a conference at the Detroit Branch, Avard asked him what plans were made for the World Fair. He knew of none, but would contact the Authorities in Salt Lake. There was still a booth available in the Hall of Religion. Plans were drawn for a display of Latter-Day Saint history and idealism. These were submitted to the First Presidency who approved.

It was too large a project for one man, and Avard called on his family for assistance. He sent for his father, John B. Fairbanks, a pioneer Utah artist, who arrived within a week at Ann Arbor, with a roll of sketches. A large vacant mansion was rented for a studio, and a series of paintings were started while Avard modeled a bas relief sculpture portraying Latter-Day Saint family life. Two beautiful stained glass panels and a couple of impressive paintings were also created by J. Leo Fairbanks in Corvallis, Oregon. Work went on from early morning to late at night, yet the impressive art work was completed and installed by the deadline.

The paintings, depicting a series of important events in church history, attracted large crowds. The young missionaries assigned to the exhibit were able to present their message in a convincing manner, and many conversions resulted.

Chicago was so pleased by the response to the World Fair generally that they decided to continue it through 1934. The Latter-day Saint display area was enlarged, and two new statues were created and added for further impact. "The Tragedy of Winter Quarters" statue was modeled in life size. A companion piece, "New Life and New Frontiers" was a contrast portraying hope. The artistic portrayal was recognized to be so effective in the missionary effort, that it was displayed at several subsequent expositions.

Years later the paintings and sculpture were set up in the Museum on Temple Square where they remained until a new museum was created. Recent World Fairs have had Latter-Day Saint exhibits following the effort which was pioneered by Avard Fairbanks demonstrating that fine art can speak with a missionary message.

The site of the Winter Quarters Cemetery did at last receive more attention. Avard was commissioned to create a heroic bronze statue of The Tragedy of Winter Quarters. Additional bronze plaques were modeled expressing both mortal sorrow and the hope of eternal life. The grounds were beautified, landscaped and now serve as a historic pioneer shrine and landmark.

Other sacred sculpture followed, including the panels at the base of the Nauvoo Temple Bell tower, the monument to the First Sunday School, The Angel Moroni on the Washington D.C. Temple as well as the Angels Moroni on the Bellevue, Washington, West Jordan, Utah, and Mexico City Temples. Mortal Moroni was placed at Manti, for it was there that Brigham Young stated that Moroni in his wanderings had dedicated the site for a temple. Two of the sculptor's most impressive statues are "The Restoration of the Aaronic Priesthood" and "The Restoration of the Melchizedek Priesthood". Their message will be an inspiration for many years to come.

If any criticism should be considered, it would be that his plans were too extensive. When asked to create a statue, he would plan a monument, not just a statue standing on a pedestal as conceived by lesser intellectuals. His creative, imaginative expression conceived sculptured figures to portray motivation toward an ideal, complemented by a surrounding stone masonry enclosure with beautiful landscaping. He felt that if an historic character, event or organization deserved recognition, the monument should serve as an inspiration to all observers.

Advancing age did not slow Avard's plans. He envisioned a monument to peace with two venerable figures looking over a blacksmith and apprentice beating swords into ploughshares, with the caption, "And he shall judge among the nations and shall rebuke many people: and they shall beat their swords into ploughshares, and their spears into pruninghooks: nation shall not lift up sword against nation, neither shall they learn war any more."

(Isaiah 2:4)

His last conceived project was a heroic statue of Saint John the Revelator looking up into the heavens. A sketch was made in clay portraying the Author in the book of Revelations, saying "And I saw another Angel fly in the midst of heaven, having the everlasting gospel to preach to them who dwell upon the earth, and to every nation, and kindred, and tongue, and people "

(Revelations 14, 6-7)

One of the last writings found on his desk deserves to be included as a philosophical admonition.

"When one proclaims a disbelief in God and his powers, then one becomes an atheist or agnostic and divorces himself from celestial support and the influences of the Holy Spirit.

He gives up his heritage and relationships with the holy family bonds and ties.

Thus one becomes spiritually alone in a physical world of greed, suspicion, and intrigue, and is subject to physical survival."

The clay and tools were lifted from the sculptors hands on the first day of 1987, at the end of a 78 year professional career. Avard Fairbanks left a legacy of influence and momentum to create high quality and dynamic art among his students and family which death cannot erase. His mission continues in bronze and stone.